SMART PARENTS
GUIDE to COLLEGE

SMART PARENTS
GUIDE to COLLEGE

The 10
most important
factors for
students and
parents when
choosing a
college

Ernest L. Boyer and Paul Boyer

Peterson's

Princeton, New Jersey

Visit Peterson's at http://www.petersons.com

Library of Congress Cataloging-in-Publication Data

Boyer, Ernest L.
    Smart parents guide to college : the 10 most important factors when choosing a college / by Ernest L. Boyer and Paul Boyer.
        p.   cm.
    Includes index.
    ISBN 1-56079-591-3
    1. College choice—United States.   2. College student orientations—United States. 3. Universities and colleges—United States.   I. Boyer, Paul, 1964-   .   II. Title.
    LB2350.5.B69   1996
    378.1'05—dc20   96-31264
                                                                                                            CIP

Editorial direction by Carol Hupping
Production supervision by Bernadette Boylan
Proofreading by Joanne Schauffele

Composition by Gary Rozmierski
Creative direction by Linda Huber
Interior design by Cynthia Boone

Printed in the United States of America

10 9 8 7 6 5 4 3 2 1

*To Kathryn, wife and mother,
and Hilary, wife and daughter-in-law.*

Contents

Acknowledgments

We are indebted to hundreds of colleges and universities around the country. Nearly 700 schools responded to our requests for information and countless individuals—administrators, faculty, and students—took time to describe their institutions in greater detail during follow-up interviews. Without their enthusiastic help, this book would not have been possible.

We also must acknowledge several people who acted as informal consultants and advisers while we were completing the book. John Gardner, director of the National Resource Center for the Freshman Year Experience at the University of South Carolina, contributed a wealth of data and a thoughtful critique of chapter 1, Getting Ready for College. Evan Farber, former head librarian at Earlham College and a national expert on academic libraries, was consulted regularly during the completion of chapter 6, Resources for Learning. Arthur Levine, president of Teachers College at Columbia University, provided guidance during the writing of chapter 3, A Curriculum with Coherence. His comments were invaluable.

Two colleagues and close friends deserve special thanks. Robert Hochstein, assistant to the president at the Carnegie Foundation, helped polish chapter 2. Lee Mitgang, a senior fellow at the foundation, made many helpful suggestions for chapters 5 and 7.

Finally, we want to thank Peterson's for its unwavering support of this project. Our editor, Carol Hupping, skillfully guided the book past hurdles with warmth and gentle good humor.

Preface

This book was first proposed nearly ten years ago. At that time, my father, then president of the Carnegie Foundation for the Advancement of Teaching, was preparing a report on the status of undergraduate education. Released in 1987, *College: The Undergraduate Experience in America*, declared the American college a "troubled institution" and called for renewed attention to the needs of students.

Although the book was written primarily for educators, it did include a brief epilogue titled "A Guide to a Good College." In it, my father offered, in a tentative way, a series of key questions consumers should ask when looking for a college or university of quality. Is there a program of orientation for new students? Is undergraduate teaching a priority? And so on.

Almost immediately, we began talking about writing a separate book specifically for parents and prospective students that would organize these questions around ten key criteria of quality and include examples from colleges and universities around the country. With it, consumers would have the ability to recognize quality, ask the right questions, and, in the end, pick a school that best met their own needs.

We were occupied by other projects, but the idea held our imagination, and, in 1994, we agreed to work together on the book. The ten criteria were refined and a letter was sent to every college and university in the country, asking for examples of excellence from each.

My father was not able to see the book finished. For several years, he had struggled with cancer and his illness progressed just as writing started. He died at the end of 1995. Yet in all respects, he is the coauthor of this book. His unique vision and priorities shaped every chapter and, I hope, every page. Key recommendations are taken directly from our many hours of discussion and his own influential writings.

In at least a small way, I also hope that the book reflects some of the genuine passion he had for education. Above all, he believed education should break down barriers and serve to bring people together. He believed teaching was among the most noble of professions. He believed colleges should be communities, ruled by civility and respect for all its members. Most of all, he believed students mattered.

"Students go to college expecting something special," my father wrote in the opening pages of the 1987 report. He believed they should not go away disappointed.

Paul Boyer
Chestertown, Maryland
June 1996

Introduction

While the final chapters of this book were being written, millions of Americans prepared for college. Through fall and winter, favorite schools were picked and applications nervously mailed. By spring, letters of acceptance were opened and final decisions made.

For most, a happy ending.

But according to news reports, this was an especially stressful year for the college bound. College admissions—a time to celebrate accomplishments and prepare for the future—has instead become what *U.S. News & World Report*'s annual college guide calls "a period of tension and anxiety" (*America's Best Colleges,* 1995). A recent front-page story in the *Washington Post* came to the same conclusion. More students are applying to top schools and, it reports, "are feeling a new level of pressure, because the competition for admission is getting stronger" (May 7, 1996). Here's what the *Philadelphia Inquirer* found: "Year by year, competition for admission into top-tier public universities is intensifying, with applications climbing despite heart-stopping price tags of $30,000 a year" (December 22, 1995).

College, once an option for an elite few, is quickly becoming a necessary credential. Nearly three quarters of those responding to a 1991 Gallup survey agreed it was "very important" to get a college degree—a 15 percent increase in just five years. And the number of Americans in college continues to climb, despite rising costs.

The pressure to attend college is now compounded by the pressure to get into the "best" college. Worried about the future, many students want what they hope will be the added advantage that comes from a name-brand institution with, it is often assumed, the best reputation and the best education. So, while most colleges scramble to fill classroom seats, a handful of hot schools are inundated with applicants. In 1996, for example, both Harvard and Princeton accepted just 11 percent of those who applied.

Were these students the lucky few? Certainly, these and other highly selective colleges and universities have an important role to play. But we have a slightly different—and more optimistic—view of higher education as a whole.

In our research for this book, we looked at nearly 700 colleges nationwide. Some were famous, others obscure. A few were highly selective, most were not. They included a small school in Maine with less than 500 students and several large public universities in California with enrollments of 15,000 or more. Not all were equally successful, but we found many examples of excellence across the spectrum. We came to two conclusions:

> First, a good school cannot be identified by reputation or selectivity alone. These are incomplete and often misleading measurements of quality.

> And second, in higher education, one size does not fit all. Diversity exists for a reason; there is no one "best" school in America.

Students, and their parents, do themselves a disservice when they limit their college search. "Many lesser-known colleges offer a solid, challenging undergraduate experience," says the 1987 Carnegie Foundation report *College: The Undergraduate Experience in America.* The key for prospective students is to keep options open." This is all well and good.

But if a college is not picked by popularity or ranking, then how? In short: What does a good college look like? And how can students find the one school that's right for them?

This book will help you answer these questions. We describe what every good college or university should do and show you how to confidently pick the one that is, for you, the very best.

The Ten Keys to Quality

Your job is to find a college or university committed to the needs of undergraduate students—those who are pursuing a bachelor's degree. These institutions, whether large or small, must provide a rich and rewarding education both in the classroom and across the campus. We believe there must be programs and services that help all students grow, succeed, and be prepared for life after graduation.

Specifically, we believe all colleges and universities should be measured against ten key criteria of quality. Here's our list:

1. *Every college or university must help students make the transition to higher education.* They should offer a program of orientation before classes begin. They should also have special freshman-year programs that introduce students to college life.

2. *All institutions must make mastery of the English language a priority.* Writing—as well as speaking and critical thinking skills—must be nurtured in all classes, not just one or two English courses.

3. *General education should be an essential part of the curriculum.* These required courses should be presented

3

in ways that reveal connections between academic disciplines and enrich each student's major.

4. *Teaching must be valued.* Every college and university must prove that undergraduate teaching is respected and that faculty members make their students a priority.

5. *Classes—even those for first-year students—should allow time for active student participation.* Small discussion classes, group projects, research, and off-campus study should be common.

6. *The library should be judged not just by the number of books it contains, but also by how well the collection meets the needs of undergraduate students.* In addition, librarians should be seen as teachers, helping students become wise consumers of information.

7. *Students should have the opportunity to learn in more flexible ways.* More and more institutions allow students to design their own majors, complete independent study projects, and study at their own pace. When carefully guided, these programs make higher education accessible to more Americans and respond to their changing needs.

8. *Colleges and universities must work hard to create safe, caring communities where all students are treated with respect.* In addition, cultural activities and extracurricular projects will also extend learning across the entire campus.

9. *All schools must offer services that support students both academically and socially.* Student health centers, psychological counseling, academic tutoring, and career planning will, at the best institutions, play an active role and reach out to all students.

10. *Colleges and universities should ask students, before graduation, to reflect on all they have learned and to prepare for life after college through senior-year seminars, research, and other projects.*

In this book, we devote a chapter to each of these key criteria and offer specific questions you should ask when investigating schools. We also include examples from nearly 200 colleges across the country that succeed in one or more ways. In most cases, information about these colleges and universities is based on written responses supplied by the schools, along with information collected during follow-up interviews with administrators, faculty, or students.

Before you begin, it is important to remember that no college is perfect. A college of quality, we believe, should value all ten categories. But even a good school has areas of weakness. Look, instead, for colleges that focus on each, excel in a few, and also satisfy your special needs and interests.

Are any of these categories more important than others? All ten are necessary, but some offer especially meaningful insights about a college's commitment to undergraduates. How well a college helps students make the transition to higher education (chapter 1) deserves special attention. Also, carefully investigate the curriculum (chapter 3), as well as the quality of teaching and the classroom climate (chapters 4 and 5). Finally, the quality of campus life (chapter 8) reveals a great deal about a school's values and the interests of its students. Again, all categories matter, but these five are critical to the success of all institutions.

We hope that this book will help you explore all your options and, like confident consumers, pick the right college for you. For the classes of 2001, 2002, and beyond, we want the transition to college to be a time of excitement and celebration.

1

Getting Ready
for College

The first day of college may be the hardest. New students arrive on campus equipped with notebooks, pens, and enthusiasm, but the transition into a whole new life can quickly turn excitement into apprehension. Left on their own, new scholars must find their way around a campus filled with strangers and navigate the often complex academic bureaucracy. It may take many weeks, or even months, to truly feel comfortable with the pace of college life.

Increasingly, college and university leaders are recognizing the importance of the first college year and are offering programs that help students make the transition into higher education. Most institutions now offer, at a minimum, a brief orientation and some academic advising for new students before classes begin. But many do much more. At some institutions, orientations are held for a full week or more and offer not only tours of the campus, but a wide range of social and academic programs. In addition, many are now offering freshman seminars and "college life" classes that cover topics ranging from study skills to good nutrition.

The value of these programs is clear. Colleges report that retention and graduation rates rise, sometimes dramatically, when they offer strong orientation programs and special courses for first-year students. Researchers have come to the same conclusion. A 1993 study by the National Resource Center for the Freshman Year Experience says succinctly, "There is overwhelming evidence that new students who participate in orientation are more likely to earn higher grades and graduate than those who do not participate."

When looking at colleges, it is worthwhile to examine the orientation and transition programs of each and give greater weight to institutions that make it an important part of a student's first year. While there are many different kinds of programs, it is relatively easy to evaluate a college's commitment and identify the best.

Starting a New Life

Liz Likens remembers her first day as a college student. She was enthusiastic about her school and arrived a week early to participate in a volleyball program. But when boxes were unloaded and it came time for her parents to leave, she broke down and cried. "I was sobbing," she recalls. "I was hysterical. I think that was the one time in my life when I felt the absolute loneliest. I'll never forget that feeling." Today, Liz is a senior at Washington College in Chestertown, Maryland, and president of the student government. But three years ago, as a young woman leaving home for the first time, she was overwhelmed by the feeling of isolation. Bright and resilient, she fought loneliness by staying busy with sports and academic work. But she now realizes that her adjustment to college life took a full year.

Every experience was new and unfamiliar. Course registration was confusing. She was surprised by a sense of freedom so unlike high school. And like most students, she worried about her ability to succeed academically. "I remember sitting in my first class and thinking, 'I'm never going to be able to do this,'" she says. Although Liz was involved in many extracurricular activities as a high school student, she was shy and a bit withdrawn during her freshman year at college. "I didn't socialize that much; going to parties wasn't my experience in high school."

Liz finally became more active during her sophomore year. She joined student organizations, began working closely with favorite faculty, and was able to call the college her home.

Although arrival at college is a cause for celebration, it may also be a time of great uncertainty. During this period of transition, all students are working hard to fit in socially and still learning what is expected academically. But they have

9

yet to fully develop a network of supportive friends and faculty. If the experience is too disorienting, and they feel there is nowhere to turn for help, a college career, just barely begun, may already be in jeopardy.

This is true not just for poor or "at-risk" students. Even the brightest and most determined—the Most Likely to Succeed crowd—are never fully prepared for college life and its different expectations. Overall, 40 percent of students who enroll in a college seeking a baccalaureate degree do not graduate. And most who drop out do so before their sophomore year.

Setting the Tone for College

It is tempting to ignore the quality of a college's orientation program when selecting a school. Understandably, prospective students are more worried about getting *into* college; few are thinking about what will happen right after they arrive. But it is during the first days—and the first year—that the tone for the entire college career is set. For some, the transition is a "make-or-break" period.

Arrival at college is, in a very real way, the start of a new life. In this chapter, we describe how a college or university can help new students make a successful transition and prepare them to succeed both socially and academically. This is the first criteria of quality.

Does the college or university give you the right information?

The transition to college begins even before the student is admitted. Every institution has an obligation to accurately describe its programs and services to prospective students and answer their questions candidly.

For anyone picking a college, there is no shortage of helpful information and free advice. Friends, parents, and guidance counselors are usually consulted. Many college guides offer an "insider's" view of campus life. Several major magazines have special editions that rank schools. Increasingly, this information is also available on computer. But the greatest amount of material comes from the colleges. Brochures, viewbooks, video tours, calls, and even personal letters can arrive like a flood. A 17-year-old about to choose a college is a very popular person, indeed.

What College Literature Should Tell You

This recruitment material is not the most influential source of information for most students. Surveys show that parents are overwhelmingly the most important advisers for graduating high school seniors. But college publications—especially the colorful, photo-packed viewbooks—still play a strong role in the college selection process. Through this literature and, perhaps, a brief campus tour, lasting impressions are formed. Prospective students learn not just what is taught or what the campus looks like, but they also get a flavor of its mood and its values. A college choice will probably be based, at least in part, on these images. In this way, orientation to college really begins long before a student arrives on campus. The transition to higher education starts as soon as he or she begins looking at colleges. It is especially important, therefore, that the information provided by a college is accurate.

What should it tell you? Begin by looking at the admissions process. Does recruitment literature list the specific requirements for admission? Also, if test scores are required for admission—such as the SAT—does the college tell students how many are admitted by quartile, so the full range of accepted scores is known? Whether the school is open admission or highly selective, students have a right to know exactly what is required.

Also look at retention rates. Does the college's literature offer these essential figures? While some universities and colleges graduate only one third or less of students who enroll, not every student leaves because they flunked out or hated the school. At public universities especially, some students take only a few courses for personal enjoyment or repeatedly stop-out before eventually graduating. On the other hand, how comfortable do you feel in a community that is this transient?

But beyond these and other useful figures, every college and university should truthfully convey its mission and philosophy. Does it celebrate its unique role, or does it try to be all things to all people? Finally, does its literature talk honestly about the role of undergraduates?

Students eagerly seek this kind of information. While most first look at specifics, such as a college's size, location, or the variety of majors offered, the final decision is often influenced by intangible qualities. Students search for a college that feels comfortable and will prepare them for life. They read between the lines when examining recruitment literature and going on campus tours, searching for meaningful clues that reveal the true character of the institution. Finding the kind of information you need to make a well-informed decision is not always easy, however. Colleges are in competition for students and want to entice candidates, not drive them away. Most colleges want to appeal to as many prospective students as possible.

Research reveals that most prospective students are looking for a college or university with a strong academic reputation. They also want an attractive campus—images of quaint, ivy-covered buildings hold special allure—and evidence that students and faculty work together. Of course, students also want to enjoy college life and look forward to social activities and a sense of community. All institutions compare themselves favorably against this ideal. If you have looked at even one viewbook, you will probably recognize these photographs: small groups of happy students socializing outside on a warm day; students strolling in front of well-maintained buildings; a student and teacher in animated conversation; and students taking part in sports, performing arts, and foreign travel. And if there is water anywhere nearby—from an ocean to a pond—you can be sure it will be featured. In contrast, you will probably not see pictures of a lecture hall filled with 600 freshmen, a snaking registration line, or decrepit residence halls.

Students are naturally skeptical of college literature; one survey found that 40 percent of prospective students doubt the honesty of recruitment information. Hoping to get a more complete picture of a college, many try to get firsthand impressions by taking campus tours. Tours can be helpful, but like viewbooks, they are usually meant to impress more than educate. One dean of admissions at an eastern university, for example, calls the route taken by prospective students at his institution the "Money Walk" and makes sure that it is well maintained and manicured.

Quoted in the higher education journal *Change*, he explains: "We know initial impressions can be lasting impressions in this don't-miss-a-trick campaign to encourage a potential student and his or her parents to believe that we have something the campus they just visited, or will visit next, doesn't have." (March/April 1994)

Clearly, full disclosure is not encouraged.

None of this is a crime; if fervent self-promotion were against the law, almost every admissions director in America would be behind bars. It also doesn't mean that college literature and campus tours should be ignored. But it does mean that students should exercise their right to critically examine and question the material that is sent. The first test of a good college is a willingness to present itself honestly and answer inquiries fully.

Few colleges deliberately mislead prospective students. Although many colleges struggle annually to fill the next freshman class, they also want those students to stay enrolled. To simply fill slots with unhappy recruits would be, at best, counterproductive. "You don't recruit a student for one year, you recruit a student to graduate," says Lynne Henderson, director of admissions at Wesleyan College in Macon, Georgia. For example, she says, "students need to know exactly what they're getting into. They need to know how much it is going to cost them and how they will pay the bills. All of this effects retention."

Campus Visits

Henderson advises prospective students to get as much information as possible by spending time on campus and, especially, talking informally with current students and faculty. In addition, a college may be judged by the willingness of its admissions staff to answer questions openly and honestly and also by its ability to create an atmosphere that *encourages* questions. "When they first arrive on campus, the environment and how they're greeted plays a big role. If it's too formal, they're not going to ask questions; they're too scared. But if it's a warm, friendly environment, they'll ask what's really on their minds."

Every college welcomes visits from prospective students, but some provide a greater variety of formal programs for the college bound. For example, many offer preorientations that involve not just a tour, but organized presentations and overnight stays. These sessions allow students to view a college and attend talks that discuss college life and the college selection process.

Canisius College in Buffalo, New York, for example, hosts a Summer Visitation Program for high school juniors. Held as a two-day event with one overnight in college residence halls, participants can learn about financial aid and the college search process. It hosts discussions with current students who talk about their experiences in higher education.

Another program is offered by the United States Naval Academy in Annapolis, Maryland. Its Summer Seminar offers a six-day session for high school juniors. This selective program includes academic workshops, physical training, and a taste of what life is like for a midshipman. Of course, the military emphasis of the academy has little in common with the rest of higher education.

Most of these preorientation programs have a strong public relations function. Colleges offering a preview program obviously hope students will like what they see and choose to apply. But they do provide opportunities to get a better understanding of college life and the character of a particular institution.

In the end, these programs only formally present what prospective students can learn on their own during campus visits to nearly every college in America. The first step is to look beyond the literature and to judge a college by its eagerness to give students all the information they need. It is appropriate to judge a college or university by how carefully and honestly it answers your questions.

Does the college or university provide a creative, well-planned program of orientation?

Every college should welcome new students when they arrive on campus. This program of orientation should include all new students and feature activities that prepare them both academically and socially. At the best orientation programs, all members of the campus community—including faculty and the president—take part.

Formal orientation begins after a student has been admitted to college. Either immediately before classes begin, or sometime during the summer, a college will sponsor a program of welcome for new students. Traditionally, these are one-, two-, or three-day events, and attendance may be optional, although participation is now mandatory on many campuses. Often there is a small charge to attend. In almost every case, an orientation will offer a variety of social activities, such as dances, pizza parties, and mountain hikes, that help students feel comfortable and make friends. At the same time, these activities help prepare students for their first semester of study. Time is usually allotted for campus tours, meetings with advisers, opening convocations, placement testing, and course registration. By the end of even the most rudimentary orientation, students should know their way around campus, have a few new friends, and be ready to attend class.

Black Hills State University in Spearfish, South Dakota, offers a new student orientation with its own distinctive flavor. But in its scope, it is typical of orientations offered at many colleges and universities around the country. The program begins in the fall, three days before the new semester. Students taking part in orientation—about 60 percent of the total freshman class—arrive *en masse* to the campus, most accompanied by family members. Meeting them is a contingent of volunteers, ranging from the university president and students to the town mayor and local shop owners. As cars pull in, students are shown where to check in and get help unloading boxes and finding their rooms. They then can relax with soft drinks donated by the

National Guard and read through literature about the university and community supplied by the local chamber of commerce.

"When students come to orientation, they think they just want information," says Sandra Cargill, director of the university's student assistance center. So the first full day is devoted to informational sessions, such as "What to Expect the First Year," "Intro to Internet," and "Distance Learning." These sessions are open to family members, and one, "The College Transition for Parents," is specifically devoted to their concerns. Later, a formal farewell is held for the families. An afternoon reception prepares families for the separation and helps students think of college as their new home.

The second day emphasizes the student/faculty relationship. Students learn how to be good advisees and make a positive impression in the classroom. "We give them dos and don'ts," says Cargill. "There are things you don't want to say. For example, if you miss class you don't say [to the professor], 'Did I miss anything?'" Manners count, too. Students are reminded to make appointments if they wish to talk with faculty—and keep them.

Next, students have an opportunity to practice their newly learned etiquette skills at a lunch with faculty. Assigned seating ensures that faculty and new students actually sit next to each other and converse—Cargill says the teachers are especially shy and have a tendency to sit away from students. Later, instructors from each department talk about their disciplines to prospective majors. Students find out not just what is required to get a degree, but also what it takes to succeed. "For example, what does it take to be a political science major?" explains Cargill. "What does the department consider to be a good student? What is that student like?" While some students arrive on campus certain of their majors and stick to them, many more are undecided. These sessions help students think more deeply about their interests and abilities.

The final day focuses on the college community and the contributions students can make to society. "Part of this is getting involved in campus activities. We try to emphasize service," says Cargill. For example, the students come up with real proposals for volunteer service and present them to the group.

Like most orientations, the program at Black Hills also offers plenty of opportunities for socializing. Each day features a dance, buffet meal, or organized group-building activity. And each year's events are organized around a theme. Recently, it featured a Western motif. There were line dance lessons, rope tricks, stick horse races, and a cookout featuring buffalo burgers and buffalo wings, all served by the president, vice president, and college deans. The finale was a Wild West show.

Cargill admits that some of the activities sound silly, but she says much of it is education disguised as entertainment. During the Western theme orientation, for example, students also learned more serious lessons about the region's western heritage and Native Americans. And even—perhaps especially—during some of the silliest of activities, students were making friends and growing comfortable with their new lives.

Certainly, this university's orientation is distinctive. Other colleges will offer programs with different activities and have a different feel. But all good programs produce similar results. Students will begin their first semester of learning feeling both at home and academically prepared.

Many other colleges offer their own unique contribution to the standard orientation program. At the University of Southwestern Louisiana in Lafayette, for example, the two-day mandatory orientation includes a mock classroom session. After a brief sample lecture, an instructor discusses appropriate classroom behavior and reviews the responsibilities of both teachers and students. Although the class takes less than an hour, it helps reduce student anxiety for the first day of real instruction. "There's a lot of fear when walking into the first class," says Jimmy Clarke, dean of enrollment management at the university. "The feeling is, 'I know what high school was, but what is this?' "

The session gives students hands-on practice. The first assignment, says Clarke, is to find the classroom—not a small problem at a university of nearly 17,000 students. Like a real class, the instructor hands out a syllabus and then presents a lecture, complete with slides or video when appropriate. After about 20 minutes, the professor stops the lecture to review the class, offer tips (a typical pet peeve: don't come late), and answer questions. Students inquire about everything from absentee policies to the acceptability of gum chewing.

Linfield College in McMinnville, Oregon, meanwhile, makes creative use of computer technology to make orientation accessible 24 hours a day. Most campus computers have access to the Linfield Companion, an on-line guide for students that describes campus services and lists student activities. It also offers advice from upperclass students and even includes a list of the faculty members' favorite books. The computer guide allows new students to find their way around campus without having to ask what they fear are stupid questions, says John Reed, dean of enrollment services.

Teaching Values

A quality orientation offers far more than "how-to" information. It is also time to teach—and practice—the values of the college. Every college is a community, and each is unique, with its own history, mission, and traditions. Orientation is often used to reinforce and celebrate what is special about the institution. Students are reminded that they are working not just to earn their individual degrees, but to help each other and build a stronger college.

High Point University in High Point, North Carolina, has organized much of its mandatory orientation around the theme of community and makes students the focus of its program. During the first of four daily convocations, the incoming class is formally presented, and individual students are profiled by the admission staff. During the last session, the students are inducted into the "Old Montlieu Society"—a new tradition that welcomes students into the campus community with a certificate and hat. "Not a beanie," vice president for internal affairs Morris Wray is quick to explain, "but a nice hat, the kind students fight over."

All of these activities reinforce Wray's conviction that orientation should be a celebration of a student's entry into higher education and should build a sense of common purpose. "The most important time is orientation," he asserts, "not graduation." Although the program at High Point University is only a few years old, Wray says it is already making a difference. He notices that students who take part become more involved in campus activities. More freshmen are in leadership roles and are choosing more rigorous classes. "They're taking part from the day they get here," he says.

Colleges and universities are also stressing the value of volunteer work, often called service learning, as part of their emphasis on community. Many schools now require students to volunteer their time before graduation, and some are making it a part of their orientation programs. Bluffton College in Bluffton, Ohio, sends students out into the surrounding community almost as soon as they arrive to work for 2 or 3 hours on one of seventeen different projects. Students may pick up trash, help build low-income housing with Habitat for Humanity, or work in a nonprofit thrift store. A few hours of work is in some ways only symbolic, but it does demonstrate to the students the college's strong commitment to social service.

Making Friends and Building Community

Most colleges offer plenty of social and recreational activities during even the briefest orientation. However, some make a special effort to challenge students physically, as well as intellectually. Salisbury State University in Salisbury, Maryland, offers an optional weeklong wilderness program. New students can chose to sail on the nearby Chesapeake Bay, cycle in Maine's Acadia National Park, or canoe in the Algonquin Provincial Park of Canada. Faculty, staff, and student counselors lead these wilderness experiences during the day and discuss the meaning of learning and community in the evening.

Unity College in Unity, Maine, makes a weeklong wilderness program a required part of its orientation. New students can hike the Appalachian Trail, canoe down the Penobscot River, or camp in Maine's Baxter State Park, among other options. Each group is limited to ten students and two group leaders, who are either upperclass students or recent alumni.

This unique program also includes a day for service projects. Hikers may help build a retaining wall, clean up a camp site, or haul wood chips to help protect a trail. Other groups may help repair beaches damaged by erosion.

These outdoor experiences are recreational but also teach important lessons. The program at Unity College, for example, helps build friendships, encourages self-reflection, and emphasizes the values of this small, environmentally aware college. "Our goal is to use the wilderness to get at issues we feel are important during the [student's] transition," says Chip Curry, who coordinates the program.

"We're not just trying to get to the destination point—to the top of the mountain or the end of the river. Students are very focused on *how* they get there," says Curry. There are daily meetings to discuss group dynamics, and time is set aside to write in a personal journal. "We are addressing how to live in a community. Students are having to think how their actions affect other people." Friendships also form, easing the transition socially. Even on their first day of school, participants will see ten familiar faces. "They're going to come into the school with a lot less anxiety," says Curry.

This spirit of camaraderie and support can be built in other ways. Chadron State University in Chadron, Nebraska, works especially hard to make new students feel at home, literally. Freshmen have the opportunity to join the university's Host Parent Program, which matches students with a family living in the community. While students live in residence halls, the host parents offer support and includes them in family activities. "The students eat dinner there, they can do laundry," says housing staff member Shelly Johns. "It's like a home away from home." These relationships often last for many years.

Getting Students Ready to Learn

All orientation programs help students adjust to the social life of the college, but many also help prepare students for learning. Orientation is also a time to practice writing and critical thinking skills that will soon be put to use.

Mini-classes and seminars are often held to discuss assigned readings, giving new students a chance to experience college-level work before classes begin. For example, Willamette University in Salem, Oregon, gives new students a summer reading assignment, which they discuss as part of a freshman seminar class that first meets during orientation.

Especially ambitious is the orientation at Eckerd College in St. Petersburg, Florida. Its required program lasts three weeks. As part of this intensive program, called Autumn Term, students, in groups of twenty, complete one academic project for credit. Their instructor is also their mentor for the first year.

Special Needs and Diversity Awareness

Finally, orientation is also a time to acknowledge special needs and cultural differences. Many colleges and universities now offer programs specifically for minorities and those with physical disabilities. Large state universities, especially, may have individual sessions for students with physical or learning disabilities, as well as for African Americans, Hispanics, Native Americans, international students, gays, lesbians, bisexuals, and more.

Increasingly, there are also programs that make all students aware of the diversity at their college or university and stress the importance of acceptance.

Brown University in Providence, Rhode Island, offers a series of workshops that examine cultural differences and the impact of stereotypes. All students, for example, take part in a mock party where they wear labels on their foreheads that identify them as a member of a different culture. While students cannot see their own labels, they do see each other's and are allowed to respond to them according to common stereotypes. The exercise helps students think about the assumptions they make about people different from themselves.

This growing emphasis on diversity has received a great deal of attention in the media and is sometimes criticized as too politically correct. But administrators argue that their goal is to create a healthy, respectful community. Many students will be entering a community far more heterogeneous than they have previously experienced. Learning to live comfortably in this setting is an important part of transition.

In the end, orientation tries to condense as much of the college experience as possible into a few days' worth of activities. A good program will give a taste of college-level learning and make students feel a welcome part of the college community. More broadly, it will help students think about their goals and responsibilities to others. In addition, orientation is a time to explain the priorities of the institution. Students learn what the college values most through the kind of programs it offers and the mood it creates. Although every program is unique, all should address these three key concerns.

There are some specific questions worth asking: Is orientation mandatory or optional? If it is not required, what percentage of students participate and what is the cost? Programs that attract less than half of new students should be more closely scrutinized. Also, find out if members of the staff and faculty take part in orientation—including the president. This participation helps build collegewide interest in the needs of first-year students.

Does the college or university continue to support students during the first year of study?

Orientation programs are a good start. But the transition to college may take a full term or more. The best colleges and universities continue to support students even after classes have started. Typically, they offer creative freshman seminars or college life classes that help build a sense of community and teach essential academic skills.

Among universities, St. Lawrence University in Canton, New York, is not large. With about 2,000 students, it looks and feels more like a liberal arts college. But all freshmen also become part of an even smaller community as soon as they arrive. For the first year, students join one of twelve "residential colleges," living and learning with forty-five other new students. Each of these mini-communities takes a common year-long class, taught by a team of three faculty members, and lives in the same university dorm.

Living and Learning Together

Every residential college class has a different theme, although all tend to focus on a social issue. Recent courses examined subjects ranging from health and wellness to the impact of mass media in society. In each case, the approach is interdisciplinary. One recent course, for example, was taught by the university's art gallery director, a writing professor, and a sociology professor. But learning is not confined to the classroom. Because students both study and live together, the distinction between their class and the rest of college life is deliberately blurred. "Learning isn't just something you do in the classroom," explains Macreena Doyle of St. Lawrence. "By living together as a community, students are going to learn together also." The First Year Program at St. Lawrence is a rich and challenging part of that institution's curriculum. Students, from their first day of class, are exploring important issues and are given the opportunity to reflect on their own values.

The program also helps set the tone for all four years of learning. Through class discussions, writing assignments, and library research, students build skills they will need during their college career. "What we really want is for students to develop their own voice and learn how to defend their own opinions," says Doyle. "We feel that is the best preparation for what they are going to do during the rest of their time here." By living and learning with a small group of students holding similar interests, an atmosphere of support is more easily established. Camaraderie is built as students collaborate and commiserate. Through this, new students more quickly become part of the whole university community.

The program at St. Lawrence University reflects a growing emphasis in higher education on the first year of learning. Too often, new students are all but abandoned after their orientation, left to fend for themselves once classes start. While upperclass students—those who have persisted—enjoy smaller classes, more attention from faculty, and take part in creative projects, new students frequently toil through large introductory classes, succeeding or failing in relative anonymity. Many also spend their first year standing on the sidelines of college life, working hard to find their niche with little support or encouragement.

Special Support for Freshmen

Many professionals in higher education now agree that this situation is no way to start a college career. New students need the most attention, not the least. While a good orientation program makes the transition easier, even the best program cannot build all necessary skills, answer every question, or anticipate each possible roadblock. So the new emphasis is on what some educators call "front-loading." The support and personal attention that was once reserved only for juniors and seniors is now being offered to freshmen. Creative interdisciplinary courses, usually taught in small classes, are being offered even in the first semester. Like the program at St. Lawrence, a special effort is made to bring students into the college community and build academic skills.

Today, 70 percent of colleges and universities offer some version of the first-year program, often called "Freshman Year Experience," "College 101," or "Freshman Seminar." While the content of these programs varies greatly, all serve to extend the support offered during orientation into the first year of learning and get students fully involved in college life. At some institutions, they are one-term elective courses. At others, they are not only required, they define the first year of study.

A growing number of colleges now feature programs similar to that offered at St. Lawrence University. Gettysburg College in Gettysburg, Pennsylvania, for example, also places freshmen in living-learning communities organized around a theme. The University of Tennessee in Knoxville has a Volunteer Community Program for students living more than 50 miles from home who have not declared a major or selected a roommate. These freshmen can live on a specially designated residence floor and take core courses together. Social events are also offered, including group dinners, a ski trip, and volunteer service projects.

Other colleges and universities do not combine classes and housing but do offer creative thematic courses. The University of North Carolina at Greensboro sponsors freshman seminars on a wide range of subjects. Topics taught in recent years have included "Technology and Life in the Ancient World," "The Making of the Atomic Bomb," and "Images of Women in the Western World." Class size is limited to twenty, and discussion, not lecture, is emphasized.

Douglass College, a women's college that is part of Rutgers University in New Brunswick, New Jersey, is starting a new program called "Examining a Life." This ten-week course looks at the lives of women through autobiography, biography, and oral history. Each week, there is a guest lecture by a woman leader—recent speakers included a poet, a corporate CEO, and a molecular biologist. Students also complete their own oral history project based on the life of an older woman in their family or community. Again, the emphasis is on building skills—reading, writing, and critical thinking. But it also stresses self-reflection. By examining the lives of women who have made a difference, students are expected to reflect on their own goals. The program is new and is not yet available to all students, but Associate Dean Ann Stehney expects that it will soon be offered to all entering students.

In these classes, students learn by doing. Students do not *study* reading, writing, or speaking. Instead, it is expected that they will gain these skills—and become active in the college community—as they work to successfully complete the course and its requirements. These classes have an academic focus and are frequently quite rigorous.

Other colleges take a different approach by stressing basic college survival skills. Each session in these "college life" courses is an opportunity to learn how to study, manage time wisely, learn about campus services, and discuss what students want from a college education. Many colleges are now encouraging students to also think about their careers and introduce them to the career center even during the first term.

Defiance College in Defiance, Ohio, offers a typical program. Its freshman seminar covers subjects ranging from peer pressure and drug use to tips on note taking and paper writing. New students are also required to take part in campus activities. "Students who get involved with college life beyond the classroom are more likely to succeed," explains program coordinator Russel Leuthold. So freshmen are expected to attend campus lectures and cultural events as part of the course's requirements. He sees that students are now more involved in campus activities even after the class ends.

Building Skills and Serving Adult Students

Like orientation, first-year programs may also cater to special needs. Some colleges have courses for students who are less academically prepared. The Catholic University of America in Washington, D.C., for example, offers a program for those who need additional help building college-level skills. Although the program, called FRESHSTART, is highly structured, it is also intensive and academic in its focus. Like many introductory courses in the humanities, it includes readings from classical literature—such as Homer's *Odyssey*—and examines paintings, sculpture, and film. Students are not taking part in a remedial course. Instead, they are carefully guided through college-level work that, like other first-year programs, prepares them for success in all their courses.

Other institutions offer programs for adult students. East Tennessee State University in Johnson City has an especially strong program for nontraditional students, providing a separate orientation program, along with counseling services and career interest testing. After enrollment, students can take a special orientation course, receive support from peer mentors, and socialize in an adult and commuter student lounge. The university also allows adult students to by-pass the confusion—and frustration—of course registration. For adult students only, the university offers a preselected list of general education courses and a reserved seat in each class. This slate of evening classes is applicable to any major.

Students don't have to struggle through the red tape of registration or be frustrated if a particular class is already full.

Missouri Southern State College in Joplin, Missouri, offers a "Return to Learn" orientation course for students who are considering entering college for the first time or whose education has been interrupted for a number of years. The course provides a basic college overview and helps rebuild study skills.

These programs are offered to adult students because they often lack confidence and are easily scared away from college, says Carla Warner, director of the Center for Adult Programs and Services at East Tennessee State. "They have a fear of appearing stupid," she says, "They're afraid they'll stick out like a sore thumb." This is not the case; nationally, nearly half of students are considered nontraditional, and at some institutions, they clearly dominate. But programs like these do build confidence and also address many of the concerns older students are more likely to face, from the need for career-change counseling to baby-sitting services.

When looking for a college, find out if the first year of study is organized around the freshman seminar. Especially attractive are programs that integrate living and learning. As an alternative, is a college life course offered? Next ask: Are these courses required? If not, what percentage of students enroll? As a general rule, a mandatory course is more likely to reflect a collegewide commitment to serving the needs of undergraduates.

Reaching Out to Meet Each Student's Needs

Some orientation programs are more comprehensive than others. However, almost every college now helps students make the transition into college in some way. Within the past fifteen years, especially, there has been explosive growth in the number of students taking orientation sessions. In 1980, 70 percent of students went through orientation. This increased to 84 percent in 1991, according to data from the National Center for the Freshman Year Experience. Even more dramatic is the growth of orientation courses and freshman seminars. In 1982, only 40 percent of colleges had an orientation class or freshman seminar. By 1992, this grew to 69 percent and continues to climb.

This is good news for students. It means nearly everyone who enrolls in a college or university will get some type of support and advice during the first year, when success or disappointment is often determined. But, more deeply, it also reflects a growing interest in the needs of students generally. It shows that college educators are acknowledging the concerns of their students and taking greater responsibility for their success.

Only since the end of World War II and especially since the mid-1960s have colleges and universities felt any responsibility to reach out to all Americans. Before then, higher education was accessible only to an elite few. These students came from the most privileged classes, shared the same values and ambitions, and were groomed for their eventual entry into college. Yet, even as college enrollment grew and a much greater variety of students enrolled, the organization of colleges and college life remained much the same. Although they were teaching the masses, they acted as if they were only educating the aristocracy. Many students enrolled, but too many felt unwelcome and out of place.

Colleges are organized for the convenience of the educators, especially the faculty, and reflect their own values, argues John Gardner, an expert on college orientation programs. "The whole structure of college was set up for

31

highly competitive, individualistic white men. That kind of a structure doesn't work well for many of the students we've been admitting.'' So educators have been working hard in recent years to understand why students succeed or fail. They are trying to offer programs that help ensure success. Orientations and freshman seminars are evidence of that effort.

When looking for a college, then, it is important to closely examine the orientation program offered. A strong program helps new students make the transition during the first days and months. In addition, it also demonstrates a genuine commitment to students. It means the school is focused on students' needs and is taking personal interest in their success. Your first day in college is an important milestone. It should be treated with respect.

The Key Questions to Ask

Transition and orientation programs set the tone for college learning. Carefully investigate how the colleges and universities you consider support new students.

1. **Does the college or university give you the information you need to make the right choice?**
   - Does it describe the specific requirements for admission—such as the range of acceptable test scores or minimum GPA?
   - Does it report retention rates and give data showing where students go after graduation? For example, what percentage find work? What percentage continue their education?
   - Does the institution's mission statement specifically mention the importance of undergraduate education?

- Does the admissions staff present the college or university honestly and answer questions fully?
- Are you encouraged to wander around campus and visit informally with students, staff, and faculty?

2. **Does the college or university provide an orientation program?**
   - Is it mandatory and free? If not, what percentage of students participate and what is the cost?
   - Does it offer an introduction to both social and acadmemic life? For example, do students take part in mini-classes or seminars. Do students formally meet with advisers and faculty?
   - Does it build a sense of community by stressing campus traditions and values? Some colleges ask new students to take part in service learning projects. Others examine the issue of diversity.
   - Are special orientation programs offered for older students, students with disabilities, or others with special needs?
   - Do all members of the college community participate in orientation—including the president, faculty, and students?

3. **Does the college or university continue to support students during their first year of study through freshman seminars or college life classes?**
   - Are they optional or required?
   - Do they integrate living and learning? If not, how do they help students become an active part of the college community?

2

Clear Writing,
Clear Thinking

Through careful reading and thoughtful writing, we think more deeply and demonstrate all that we know. Appropriately, English is one of the first subjects most students study in college. Today, more than 85 percent of American colleges and universities require their students to complete at least one English course, making it the most common required general education class.

But the best institutions offer much more. Writing, along with reading and speaking, are part of the whole college experience. They are used by students in all majors and during all four or more years of study. In other words, language is not just one more subject to study—like history or math—but is used to teach and explain all disciplines.

Many colleges and universities offer officially designated "writing-intensive" courses. Some expect students to write in nearly every class. Many feature language skills both at the beginning of college, through interdisciplinary freshman seminars, and at the end, with senior seminars and research papers. Others help those who need to build basic skills or sponsor a wide variety of student publications that encourage not just writing across the curriculum, but communication across the campus.

These institutions also have writing centers staffed with trained tutors who help guide students through the research and writing process and help teach faculty how to make writing a meaningful part of their classes.

The Power of Language

Writing is for English majors. Speaking is for speech majors. No need to bother with those subjects if you study engineering, right? Wrong, says Professor Aaron Krawitz. He thinks college students should use these skills in every class.

He is not, as you might suspect, a sour literature professor in a tweed coat. Instead, he is something called a material scientist, and he teaches in the engineering department at the University of Missouri–Columbia. He works with students interested in the latest technology, not in poetry, novels, or sentence structure.

But that's the point, Dr. Krawitz says. Writing is not just about grammar or literature, it's about communication. It is a tool used by all professions, including his, to explain necessary information and present new ideas. In fact, reflecting a small bias toward his own discipline, he argues that "the average engineer writes more than the average English major graduate." Those who write well are more likely to get ahead in their jobs—and in life.

Many educators agree with Dr. Krawitz. At the University of Missouri, he is joined by more than sixty instructors who offer special writing-intensive courses. These classes are taught throughout the university in disciplines ranging from fine arts to math and computer science. In fact, every student, no matter his or her major, must complete at least two writing-intensive courses to graduate. "The writing-intensive concept has to do with expression and clarity of thought, not with diagramming sentences," Krawitz says. "The idea is to ask students to express themselves through writing because it forces them to think clearly."

The program at this university is part of a much larger movement in higher education to put the spotlight on writing skills. Also stressed is critical thinking—the ability to examine and understand complex ideas, not just memorize facts.

Colleges focus on language because they know their students will not succeed after graduation if they cannot communicate. Employers, especially, are growing critical of new graduates and the colleges that teach them. Students may know theory, they say, but too many lack the necessary writing and speaking skills. It is not enough to graduate with a business degree, for example, if you cannot write a clear memo or make a persuasive sales pitch.

The benefits are felt long before graduation. When writing and speaking is built into the curriculum, students think more deeply about the subjects they study, and the whole college experience is richer. A multiple-choice test reveals a superficial understanding of some facts. But the act of writing requires students to systematically organize information and, in the process, discover what they really know—and what they do not.

A student at the University of Missouri explains: "You learn more. When I have to sit down and write a paper, I take time to think about it. In classes where we take tests, I just cram and forget most of what I learned."

Author William Zinsser puts it another way in his book *Writing to Learn*:

> Putting an idea into written words is like defrosting the windshield. The idea, so vague out there in the murk, slowly begins to gather itself into a sensible shape. Whatever we write—a memo, a letter, a note to the baby-sitter—all of us know this moment of finding out what we really want to say by trying in writing to say it.

When evaluating colleges, look for institutions that do more than offer one or two required English courses. A good college will make reading, writing, and critical thinking part of each student's whole college experience. While this may sound intimidating, the rewards are real.

Are English language skills formally taught during the freshman year?

Language should be a priority during the first year of study. Every college should offer a required English course or teach reading and writing through the freshman seminar.

Courses that focus on writing, reading, and speaking should be a part of every new student's class schedule. This is not a happy thought for some students. Many have lost all interest in English by the time they enter college, convinced that the emphasis will be on illogical grammar rules and tedious writing exercises. Instructors are aware of their reputations as nitpickers. "Our students, and much of the population, believe that the English teacher's job is to sniff out error and to punish students for it," acknowledges Laurence Musgrove, director of composition at the University of Southern Indiana in Evansville.

Students are also convinced by the time they enter college that writing is a talent possessed by only a fortunate few. It is not seen as a skill that can be taught or learned. Writers are born, not made, many feel, so why bother with an English class? "Our culture doesn't promote the idea that writing is possible for everyone," Musgrove says. "They see it as something that newspaper people do, or people with a God-given gift." But when taught well, these courses rebuild lost confidence and teach essential skills. At the introductory level, classes should emphasize the elements of clear and persuasive writing. They will develop research skills and help students learn how to analyze information in sophisticated ways.

Traditionally, these skills are developed in English composition courses taught by English faculty or writing instructors. At the University of Southern Indiana, for example, all new students enroll in "English 101," where writing and critical thinking skills are nurtured. At the College of New England in Henniker, New Hampshire, freshmen complete a year-long "College Writing" course. In this class, students also learn how to develop a research paper and follow accepted style rules. Similar courses are offered at institutions throughout the country. Some colleges, however, have eliminated this introductory course. They argue that the skills being stressed—reading, writing, speaking, and critical thinking—can be taught through other classes, especially the freshman seminar.

As described in chapter 1, first-year seminars are academic courses that help students make the transition to college. Typically, they examine an interesting topic—social, political, or historical—and stress the use of college-level skills. Language is one of those essential skills, so it is a major part of many seminars.

Some freshman seminars put a special emphasis on language. At Bryn Mawr College in Bryn Mawr, Pennsylvania, students enrolled in its year-long course read extensively and finish a paper every week. They also meet individually with their professors every other week to discuss their writing. While the seminar is not a course in English, the emphasis on reading and writing is so strong that it satisfies Bryn Mawr's English composition requirement.

Gustavus Adolphus College in St. Peter, Minnesota, offers a first-term seminar created specifically to develop language skills. There, class sizes are kept small—the limit is sixteen—and each section investigates a different theme on subjects ranging from American history to computer science.

Whether taught formally through an English composition class, or integrated into a freshman seminar, written and oral communication should be a priority during the first year of study. When investigating colleges, make sure writing skills are formally taught through these or similar courses.

Is writing and speaking required in every subject during all years of study?

Writing and speaking should be stressed throughout the curriculum. Increasingly, colleges and universities are making it a requirement in all disciplines. Language is a priority from the freshman to senior years.

Within the past ten years, especially, colleges have reintroduced writing requirements not just in the first year, but throughout all four or more years of study. Many schools now ask students to complete at least one or two classes where writing papers and presentations are formal requirements.

At the University of Missouri–Columbia, students begin writing their first semester in a required English composition course. But to graduate, they must also complete two writing-intensive courses—one in their major. Nearly seventy-five writing-intensive courses are offered at the university on subjects ranging from American art to invertebrate zoology.

Students must complete twenty pages of writing in each writing-intensive class, says Martha Townsend, director of the university's writing program. But, more important, writing also has to be part of how the class is taught. Assignments are spread out over the course of a semester, not completed in one long paper. "There won't be a humongous term paper that the faculty member assigns on day one and then collects at the end of the semester," she says. "In other words, the faculty member is going to be involved in the writing process with the students."

Writing-intensive programs are now common in America's universities. The University of Wyoming in Laramie, for example, has nearly identical requirements, beginning with a freshman-year composition course, followed by two writing-intensive classes. The University of North Carolina at Greensboro also offers writing-intensive classes in all departments. Classes are small—around twenty-five students—allowing faculty to work more closely with individual students. Many smaller colleges also feature writing-intensive courses. Gustavus Adolphus College, for example, was one of the first to offer writing-intensive courses.

These courses demonstrate a genuine commitment to language and critical thinking. But do they make a difference? Most instructors believe they do. "Students get better at expressing themselves," observes Aaron Krawitz. "They learn to focus on the important issues, and they learn how to think about problems." These skills help students succeed in his class and, he believes, in other classes.

Emphasizing Writing in Every Class

Writing can be stressed in other ways. At some colleges, because of their small size and educational philosophy, every class becomes writing intensive. Eugene Lang College in New York City takes advantage of its size—only 350 students—by keeping class sizes small and making writing and speaking a significant part of every class. Although two freshman-year writing seminars are required, the focus on language is pervasive in all subjects. Classes at this college—which focuses on the social sciences and humanities—are limited to just fifteen students.

According to Jennifer Gill Fondiller, director of admissions, "this has a profound impact on students' ability to use . . . language as a means of expression, as a way to test ideas, and as a way to build learning collaboratively."

King College in Bristol, Tennessee, focuses on language through a curriculum that includes the study of classical and modern literature. Students write and discuss what they have read and even make creative use of the visual arts. First-year students, for example, may find themselves reading writers from Homer to African-American author Zora Neale Hurston. They respond by writing essays, presenting speeches, and making group presentations. In the past, students have also rewritten and performed *Everyman,* a sixteenth-century morality play, using modern language and situations. Sophomores, taking a great books course, have presented mock news broadcasts from Camus's plague-stricken city of Oran, constructed board games based on Dante's *Inferno*, and evaluated the use of evidence in the movie *JFK*. In each of these programs, educators stress the practical value of their writing emphasis: If you can express yourself clearly and persuasively, you will be more successful in your chosen career.

At least one college has taken this argument to the next logical step by combining two formerly separate programs— business and economics—with a third, communications. The newly formed Department of Communication Arts/Business and Economics at Hastings College in Hastings, Nebraska, was created to better prepare students for the workforce. "We spent a lot of time talking to executives and confirmed that this is what they wanted from graduates," says department chair Roger Doerr. "They said, 'We need people who can close a sale, people who are comfortable with all forms of communication.'"

Within this unique department, students choose from eight majors and four minors, ranging from communication arts and journalism to accounting, economics, and business administration. All students in the department take courses in speaking and writing. In addition, students must complete two intensive writing workshops, another communication workshop or lab in their senior year, and at least one elective course in either speaking or writing.

Publications and Programs for Creative Expression

Writing skills can be developed in other ways. A college that cares about language will support writing and speaking across the campus, not just in the classroom. It will offer a rich variety of student-run publications and invite authors to campus for talks and readings. While almost every college sponsors a newspaper and yearbook, many offer more. They may also have literary journals, radio stations, and television stations. Increasingly, computers are becoming part of this communication network and a form of creative expression. At Guilford College in Greensboro, North Carolina, for example, students are designing and constructing the college's World Wide Web site on the Internet.

Willamette University in Salem, Oregon, now sponsors a writer-in-residence. These visiting writers spend time on campus presenting readings and teaching writing classes. They even help counsel students in the writing center, bringing their expertise to students in all departments, not just those interested in fiction or poetry. "We hope to overcome the division academics so often make between creative and other kinds of writing," says Carol Long, who teaches in the university's English department. "Anyone's writing can be improved by taking advantage of different strategies and ways of thinking."

When investigating colleges and universities, look for a similar commitment to language. Is it reflected throughout the curriculum? For example, are writing-intensive programs offered, or is writing integrated in other ways? Is reading assigned and critically examined? Also, are there ample opportunities to hone skills through campus publications and other media? Is the art of speaking and writing supported through public readings, writer-in-residence programs, or other activities?

So far, the emphasis has been on written communication. Yet, oral communication should also be a priority. The best colleges and universities help students become skillful readers, writers, and speakers.

Developing Public Speaking Skills

Speaking is a natural part of many writing-intensive programs and any strong liberal arts curriculum. Freshman seminars are often organized around informal class discussion and student-led presentations. This kind of active participation helps students become confident and articulate speakers.

Many colleges also offer courses that focus on public speaking skills. Virginia Union University in Richmond, Virginia, for example, offers a required public speaking course. There, students learn to organize and present a persuasive speech. The value of this class becomes most clear to students after graduation, explains W. Weldon Hill, dean of the college of arts and sciences. Employers across all professional fields want to hire graduates who can read, write, think critically, "and, of course, speak persuasively." These skills, he says, matter more than the actual degree earned. In other words, many employers would rather hire an art major who can write and speak with clarity than a business major who can do neither.

Whether taught formally as a public speaking course, nurtured informally through class discussion, or both, speaking skills should also be emphasized. When examining a college or university's commitment to language, find out how oral communication is supported.

In the end, what matters most is not the kind of writing program offered, but whether all students are expected to build language skills during all four or more years of education. The question to ask, then, is not simply, "Do you have a writing-intensive program?" Instead ask, "How do you build reading, writing, speaking, and critical thinking skills for all students?" Every college should make language a priority in every discipline and, ideally, nearly every class.

Are trained writing tutors available to students?

A good college or university sponsors trained tutors or writing centers staffed by faculty or other professionals, where students can find expert advice while completing class writing assignments.

It's eleven at night. A student is sitting in front of a computer, fingers on the keyboard, but staring at a blank screen. A paper is due tomorrow, but he doesn't know how to begin. Where can he go for help?

If this student attends Purdue University, he might only have to walk down the hall or tap a few keys on the computer. Through its innovative writing lab, advice comes to students in their dorms, over the phone, and through e-mail. Trained tutors occasionally make house calls to dorms, allowing students easy access to expert advice while they work to complete writing assignments. Through the lab's Internet site, students can send for more than 100 handouts on writing skills or ask specific questions on-line about the writing process. Students can also call the Grammar Hotline with questions. "Our theory is that you help a writer in progress," says Muriel Harris, director of the Writing Lab. "We've been looking for ways we can reach out and be available to students."

Polishing Skills at Writing Centers

Many colleges that stress writing, including most of the institutions described in this chapter, sponsor their own version of the writing lab. Students can get help understanding an assignment, finding research material, and organizing the final document. In many cases, staff members also work closely with faculty members, helping them integrate writing into their courses and come up with more interesting and effective assignments.

Harris says most students don't need help figuring out comma rules. Instead, tutors spend most of their time helping students understand the instructor's assignment. "They often come in helpless because they don't know what they are supposed to be doing. Getting them started is a major effort." Writing Lab staff members help students think about the assignment and consider the needs of their audience— offering the support they need to write the first sentence.

The biggest task is making sense of the information students collect. Having too much is often worse than having too little. "They go through the collection of information stage. They come with all kinds of note cards. But they cannot get back to the larger picture," Harris says. The tutor's task is to help students "sift through that information, figure out what to do with it, how to present it to somebody else." This, she says, is an increasingly urgent task. Computers can bring more information into a dorm room than exists in an entire library. But if it is not used carefully, students—and all writers—can become quickly lost in a sea of data and distracting trivia. Tutors can help put students back on track.

Writing centers are important, Harris says, because faculty often don't have the time needed to sit down with students individually. In addition, Writing Lab staff members seem more approachable to many students. "When students are sitting there with a nice friendly tutor and the popcorn is popping in the background, it becomes a very informal setting because we're not their teachers. There's nothing to be lost by chatting with us."

Writing centers play an especially important role at colleges and universities with writing-intensive courses. The University of Missouri, for example, has a writing lab just for students enrolled in these classes. Tutors are not only familiar with the writing process, they are also familiar with the specific courses students take. Tutors meet with faculty to discuss their assignments and have access to syllabi and assigned textbooks. In this way, they are well equipped to help students with their assignments.

Writing center staff members always emphasize that they serve all students, not just those who are poor or inexperienced writers. Professional authors know that a good editor can make their writing better; they can take a fresh look at a manuscript and identify problems the author has missed. Likewise, even well-written student papers can be made even better with the help of writing center tutors.

In fact, better students are the ones most likely to use the service of a writing center, says Jerry Fisher, director of the writing center at Washington College in Chestertown, Maryland. "Usually the less successful students don't take full advantage of it. The ones who come most often are really pretty competent and do well." Still, she says there is a misperception that writing centers exist only for students who are in trouble. "We have to clarify to students that this isn't a proofreading service, it isn't a ghostwriting service, and it isn't a remedial center."

At Washington College, the value of the writing center is most strongly emphasized during the sophomore year when all students are asked to complete a series of one-on-one conferences with writing tutors. Papers being completed for regular classes are brought in and discussed in three or more meetings. According to Fisher, this ensures that all students become acquainted with the writing center and helps dispel any stigma attached to it.

Are remedial classes offered for students needing to build basic English skills?

Many colleges help students lacking essential skills. Every college should offer placement testing for new students and provide intensive remedial training for those who arrive unprepared for college-level writing.

Students often worry that they are unprepared for college. But most colleges offer classes for those who need extra help. These courses emphasize the fundamentals of clear and correct writing, but they do not have to be tedious review sessions, where students complete workbook exercises. At Quinnipiac College in Hamden, Connecticut, all students enroll in the required freshman writing course. Those who need additional help take a special section that has identical assignments but meets more frequently. According to Mary Segall, coordinator of freshman English, these students "read the same texts, write the same assignments, and follow the same syllabus." In this way, they earn credit for the course and keep up with other students in their class.

English proficiency has special meaning to many students at Hunter College in New York City. At that institution, nearly half of its students are not native speakers of English, and more than sixty different languages are represented. Out of necessity, Hunter offers a broad range of developmental English courses, but unlike many "basic English" classes or traditional English as a second language instruction, connections are made to the entire curriculum.

For example, a course titled "English for Bilingual Students" is paired with a class taught by the classics department called "The Greek and Latin Roots of English." Students build their vocabulary while considering the similarities and differences between English and other languages. Students read selections from challenging texts, including Plato's *Phadreus*, in which Socrates tells the story of the invention of the alphabet.

Not all students need this kind of support. But for those who arrive at college not fully prepared, many good institutions offer creative, academically strong courses.

Educators often focus on the practical rewards of language. When students are taught to write and speak with confidence, they learn more and are better prepared for the world of work. But the power of language is deeper and even more profound. In a fundamental way, language defines who we are. It is how others come to know us and also how we understand ourselves and all that we experience. Through language, we communicate and comprehend. With the use of its symbols, we identify, for example, an emotion or recall the beauty of a landscape. When asking ourselves how we feel, our answer arrives in the shape of words—our memories are held and recaptured through the symbol system of language.

College should nurture this vital skill because it is also through language that we continue to learn, grow, and contribute. Through the written and spoken word, we are connected to others. Without language, we are isolated and powerless.

The Key Questions to Ask

How is English emphasized at the colleges and universities you consider? All say they make language a priority. But all have different expectations. Some merely "encourage" faculty to devise writing assignments. But others have specific writing and speaking requirements.

1. **Are writing, speaking, and critical thinking taught during the first year of study?**
   • Are one or more English composition courses required? Alternately, are these skills formally developed in a freshman seminar or similar course?

2. **Is language emphasized in all classes during all four or more years of study?**
   • Are writing-intensive classes offered? How many are required for graduation?
   • Is writing a part of most—perhaps all—courses?

3. **Are trained tutors, or the resources of a writing center, available to students needing help?**
   • What services do trained tutors offer?
   • How accessible are they to students?

- Are faculty formally helped in their efforts to make writing a part of their courses?

4. **Are placement testing and remediation offered for students lacking college-level reading and writing skills?**

3

A Curriculum
with Coherence

When looking at a college, pay special attention to its program of general education. Those with a carefully planned sequence of general education courses offer a richer and more rewarding education. At these institutions, "gen ed" is more than a grab bag of required classes that students try to get out of the way. Instead, it becomes the heart of undergraduate learning, revealing how the different branches of knowledge are connected.

Also look closely at each institution's requirements for the major. No matter what students study—no matter how specialized or vocational the subject—the major should teach more than a set of technical skills. Every major should also explore the ethical, historical, and social dimensions of its field. In this way, the best institutions ask students to reflect on the deeper meaning of their work and lives.

In this chapter we talk about the value of both general and specialized education. But we also feature colleges that try to bring these different and often competing pieces of the curriculum together in innovative ways. At these institutions, general education and the major complement each other.

Why is this important? Students educated with both depth and breadth graduate with a deeper understanding of themselves and their world. They leave prepared for their first job. But, of greater importance, they have the knowledge and skills needed to adapt to changes in this quickly changing society.

Why Go to College?

When Shirley Ellis graduated from high school in 1977 she went straight to work. For the next fourteen years she supported herself and, in time, her young daughter as a waitress and bartender. But she also hoped to get more from life. "I always wanted to go to college," she says, "but I never knew what to study." She briefly considered, then rejected, nursing. Years later Shirley finally found her true calling. "I was always good with my own finances. I purchased my own home. I was good with numbers at work—adding the tickets. So I thought accounting was what I should go into." With a clear goal in mind, she enrolled at Saint Joseph's College in Rensselaer, Indiana, determined to start a new career. She kept waitressing, but still managed to study full-time. Four years later she graduated with an accounting degree and is now employed by a nearby CPA firm.

Preparing for a Career

College is expensive and time-consuming. For some, it's a true hardship. So why bother? Shirley Ellis has a simple reply: a job. Preparing for a new career was the single greatest motivation for attending college. Most prospective students agree. Surveys of graduating high school seniors find that 75 percent believe preparing for work is an important reason to attend college. Nearly as many also say a degree should help them earn more money.

Shirley knew exactly what she wanted to study. But even students who enroll right out of high school and are undecided about their major see higher education as, above all, a path to work. Indeed, many say they would skip college altogether if it didn't help them get a better job. After all, isn't that what college is all about? The answer is a qualified yes; there's more to the story. If college offered only training for a specific career, then Shirley would have taken nothing but accounting classes and gained little more than a set of technical skills.

But Shirley wanted something else. Although she was motivated, first, by a desire to learn new job skills, she also expected higher education to give her more. "I was looking at getting some polish," she explains, "and becoming more well-rounded." She didn't know exactly what this meant, or how it would be accomplished. But she did believe that college would expose her to new ideas, and that this, too, would be valuable. "I come from a blue-collar family—even my aunts and uncles. They were either farmers or blue-collar workers," she explains. "I wanted to know how to operate in the white-collar world."

Education is viewed as a financial investment. Graduates are expected to earn back, with interest, all that they put in. But is that the only reason people go to college? Most prospective students say no; while employment may top their list of reasons, they hope college will also offer other rewards.

Preparing for Life

Shirley Ellis, like most students, believes the opportunity for self-discovery and intellectual growth is also an important reason to attend college. Nearly three quarters of the surveyed students said learning about things that interested them was a priority, according to extensive, nationwide data collected by the Higher Education Research Institute at the University of California at Los Angeles in 1994. Fifty-nine percent believed the opportunity to "gain a general education and appreciation of ideas" should be part of the college experience. While most students feel the need to prepare for work, they also want to prepare for life.

Research confirms that a college education can satisfy both. On average, college graduates are better prepared to enter the job market. "Compared with those who have not gone to college, college graduates know more, hold better jobs, make more money, [and] are more efficient consumers," reports George Kuh, after reviewing twenty years of research on the outcomes of college (*The Journal of College Admissions,* Spring 1985). But graduates are also better prepared to understand and contribute to society as a whole. Kuh also found that graduates are, as a group, politically aware, socially involved, and "more satisfied with their lives."

In this way, higher education meets two distinct needs. On one hand, it must keep in step with the latest career trends, providing training for work in the twenty-first century. On the other, it is expected to keep alive knowledge that may have first emerged centuries ago and encourage students to be educated in the broadest sense.

Picking a Major

Specialization comes through the major; when students "declare a major," it means they intend to focus on one particular subject. And their choices are almost limitless. There are more than 6,000 distinct majors offered in America's colleges and universities, from engineering and education to Slavic languages and food service management. The popularity of these programs rises and falls over time, but career-oriented degrees now top the list.

In recent years, especially, students are more likely to choose a major that appears to make them more employable. The percentage of majors in business, engineering, health professions, and assorted technical fields, for example, has risen sharply. Meanwhile, the percentage of students majoring in English, history, art, and other liberal arts disciplines has dropped. For most students, the opportunity to specialize is the best part of college. At last, they have a chance to study what they want and prepare in a tangible way for their future. "What's your major?" is probably the most common question asked in college because it helps reveal something about the student and what he or she hopes to become.

But the major is—literally—only part of the college experience. Most students will complete about forty classes before they graduate, but in a typical program less than half are in the major. What about the rest? This space is filled with electives—courses of the students' own choosing—and a set of classes collectively called general education.

A Place for General Education

General education introduces students to the breadth of the liberal arts—English, art, philosophy, the sciences, history, and more. In contrast to the specialized and often technical training found in the most popular majors, general education is seen by many as the heart of an undergraduate education. It is the part of the curriculum that encourages students to learn not just a skill, but a deeper understanding of themselves and their world.

And this offers other, more practical rewards. In fact, some argue, skills learned as a natural part of a good general education program are the most enduring and are the most desirable to many employers. For example, those who can solve problems and adapt to new situations are the ones who are happiest and most successful in work.

These, then, are the two parts of American higher education. Each is important; one is incomplete without the other. In this chapter we help you identify institutions that recognize the importance of both and, especially, understand that, in the end, general and specialized education must support one another. These colleges demonstrate, in the words of one university catalog, "the essential unity and wholeness of knowledge." They will also offer what we call an "enriched major," where students are asked to explore the meaning and implications of their degrees.

Is general education a priority?

Ninety-five percent of American colleges and universities have some form of general education. But some make it an especially meaningful part of the curriculum. At these schools, students are carefully guided in their selection of general education classes and may complete a "core" of required classes. In addition, these courses are taught not just in the first two years of college, but continue from the freshman to senior year.

At the best colleges and universities, general education is a true priority. At these schools, general education courses reveal how all knowledge is connected and relevant to students' lives. Students become more than "well rounded." They leave with a new and deeper understanding of themselves and their place in the world.

Writing to a group of undergraduates nearly twenty years ago, the late Charles Frankel, former chairman of the National Center for the Humanities, said: "If you have a liberal education, you will live at more than one level. You won't simply respond passively to events, and you won't be concerned with them only personally. At least sometimes you will see your fate, whatever it is, as an illustration of the human condition and the destiny of man." General education should be the part of the curriculum that encourages this kind of insight.

General Education with a Guide

How can you tell if general education is a priority at the schools you consider? First, look for a college or university where students are carefully guided in their selection of general education courses, through a core of required classes, a limited selection of optional courses created specifically for the general education curriculum, or a combination of the two. At these schools, general education is more than a random collection of courses that satisfy loose "distribution requirements"; it is coherent, relevant—and interesting.

A quick examination of a college's course catalog will help you pick the best institutions. Find out, first, how many general education classes are offered, advises Arthur Levine, president of Teachers College at Columbia University and coauthor of *A Quest for Common Learning*. "Avoid any school that has a list of possible [general education] courses longer than your arm," he proposes. When students pick from a large menu of optional courses, cafeteria style, essential connections are too often lost.

Look, too, at the titles of general education classes. Do they appear to be connected to each other? Are they presented in a logical sequence? If not, says Levine, "you can bet the requirements have not been carefully thought out."

Finally, it is worthwhile to ask students a few questions. How do they feel about general education? Is it something to get out of the way? Or do they feel that it does, in fact, make their experience richer and more meaningful? Even a good program of general education may not be fully appreciated by current students, but graduates may have a more complete perspective. They can tell you if general education courses made a difference in their lives. A college should give you names of graduates willing to answer these and other questions.

Where General Education Works

At most colleges and universities students fulfill general education requirements—typically in math, English, art, philosophy, and perhaps a few other areas—by picking from a list of optional classes taught within the different academic areas. The best programs, however, offer a *limited* number of courses that, preferably, have been created specifically for the general education curriculum.

This approach is followed at Harvard University in Cambridge, Massachusetts. All undergraduates are now expected to complete eight courses from ten areas that reflect the breadth of the liberal arts. science, literature and arts, moral reasoning, and more. Students choose the courses they prefer (one from each area), but pick from a list of just 100 options that, in most cases, have been developed specifically for the general education program.

Alternately, other schools may supplement distribution requirements with one or more "core" courses. For example, Columbia University in New York City requires all students to satisfy distribution requirements in science, foreign language, physical education, and non-Western cultures by picking from a carefully chosen list of approved classes. But at the heart of the general education program is a set of four required courses. The oldest, "Contemporary Civilization," was first introduced in 1919 and has been called the "granddaddy" of all such general education classes. It is a year-long examination of Western civilization's religious, political, and moral philosophies. Students begin by reading Plato's *Republic* and move on to the writings of Aristotle, Machiavelli, Rousseau, Darwin, Virginia Woolf, and more. In each case, the course stresses relevance to modern problems.

Less common is the true core curriculum where all students take the same general education classes. At these schools, undergraduates complete as many as ten or more core classes, usually in the same order. Saint Joseph's College in Rensselaer, Indiana, has a model core curriculum. In fact the whole sequence of required general education classes is simply called "Core." There, all students complete ten required courses, spread over all four years of study. Together, students and faculty examine, in a carefully organized sequence, history, science, philosophy, and different cultures. The curriculum stresses how each influences the other and how this knowledge can be applied to the student's major.

For example, "Core One," the first course taught in the freshman year, looks at modern American history. It meets five days a week—twice in a large hall where all freshmen gather for a formal lecture and three times in small discussion classes with just fifteen to eighteen other students. It is a 6-credit course—the equivalent of two regular classes—and fills nearly half of the students' course schedules. "Core Two" is taken by freshmen during their second semester. It steps back farther in time and studies the seventeenth to the twentieth centuries, examining not just historical events, but also the values of each era and how they were expressed. "We're doing everything rolled into one—literature, philosophy, religion, history, political science," says Parker Bernard, vice president for academic affairs.

During the sophomore year students study the Greeks and Romans, examining the roots of Western civilization. In the third year, students also take "Core Science," which examines the scientific method through reading, discussion, and hands-on work in the lab. They also study non-Western cultures. In their senior year, the core curriculum ends with an exploration of the Christian faith, encouraging students to think about their own beliefs.

A few other colleges have a similar program of study. Mount Saint Mary College in Emmitsburg, Maryland, for example, offers a sequence of twenty core courses spread over all four years of learning. Half of each student's course load is reserved for these classes. "All students take the same classes and basically in the same order," says William Meredith, dean of undergraduate studies.

These four schools reflect different approaches to general education. Yet each represents a serious commitment to liberal learning. We encourage you to look for schools that follow one of these approaches, and pick the one that reflects your own needs and interests.

Making Room for General Education

At Harvard, general education occupies about one quarter of a student's time. At some colleges is takes up even more space. The core curriculum at Mount Saint Mary College consumes about half of undergraduate learning—an unusual commitment. However, at many institutions general education is losing ground. When given the choice, many students prefer to take classes related to their major, and many are also attracted to double majors, which means double specialization. All this works against general education.

Do the colleges and universities you consider show their commitment to general education by putting limits on how many courses students may take in their major? Do they discourage double majors (although minors are common and can complement the major)? General education is an essential part of a liberal arts education. It should not have to compete for the time and attention of students.

General Education from the Freshman to Senior Year

Finally, general education should continue during all years of learning. Not something to "get out of the way" in the first year or two of study, it should complement the major and help students prepare for life after college. For example, at both Saint Joseph's College and Mount Saint Mary College, core courses continue into the junior and senior years. Other schools may offer a series of three or four core classes—one a year— that examine a different theme each year. Freshman seminars (discussed in chapter 1) and senior seminars (discussed in chapter 10) are another way to extend general education across all years of study.

Is general education a part of each student's schedule during all years of study? Or are students expected to complete general education during the first two years?

Is general education taught outside the classroom and off campus?

Campuswide seminars and even off-campus travel is made a formal part of general education at some institutions.

General education is not always taught in a classroom. It can take place across the campus and may even be pursued away from campus. Some colleges and universities enrich their general education curriculum with campuswide lectures and cultural events, such as film presentations and travel to museums.

Every semester students enrolled in core courses at Holy Names College in Oakland, California, present a campuswide festival. For example, they have organized Renaissance and Medieval fairs in the semester when this part of Western history was being studied. Booths are constructed across campus for demonstrations of everything from calligraphy to palm reading, and skits are presented on stages. In addition, students are also required to go off campus and attend three cultural events—such as concerts and plays—that some way make connections to the content of the college's general education curriculum. Administrators note that this is not a difficult task; the San Francisco Bay Area is rich with cultural offerings.

General Education Abroad

Some colleges ask students to go even farther off campus. Goshen College in Indiana, for example, requires nearly all of its students to spend thirteen weeks studying and working in one of six countries. Sites include Costa Rica, the Ivory Coast, and even China. The college was, in fact, the first to offer an undergraduate program to China. Students, traveling in groups no larger than twenty three, spend their first six weeks in the country's capital or other major city. They study the language and live with host families. Accompanying faculty, meanwhile, arrange lectures and field trips that investigate the nation's natural science and culture. During the second six weeks, the focus is on work. "For this we usually send them out of the capital into rural areas," says Wilbur Birky, director of international education. "They may work as assistants in hospitals, teaching English in schools, sports programs, construction—a whole array."

The Goshen Study-Service Term is not just three months of foreign travel. It is a carefully organized part of the college's core curriculum. "It is gen ed," says Birky. "It is core." Through their study and work students earn credit in language, social science, humanities, natural science, and more.

Most colleges offer opportunities for off-campus study. However, this program specifically supports the general education curriculum. Are similar opportunities offered at the colleges or universities you are considering?

Does the college or university offer an "enriched" major?

Every major, even the most specialized, should teach more than a set of technical skills. An enriched major will also explore the history and social implications of its field.

Nearly every student must declare a major, usually during the sophomore or junior year. Most students have a hard time choosing. No wonder: even a small college may have dozens of distinct majors, and a large university may offer more than a hundred. And more majors are added every year. Some respond to changing student interests, such as environmental studies and gender studies. But most new majors reflect the growing specialization of careers. It is now possible, for example, for those interested in business to major in everything from "business education" to "foods and nutrition in business." Disciplines are being sliced into smaller and smaller pieces.

Students have the right to pick a major that satisfies their interests and leads to a desired career. But every major must also have what the Carnegie Foundation report, *College*, calls "legitimate intellectual content" with the capacity to "enlarge, rather than narrow, the vision of students." It explains:

> If a major is so narrow and so technical that it cannot be discussed in terms of its historical and social implications, if the work in the proposed field of study cannot be a broadening experience, then the department is offering mere technical training that belongs in a trade school, not on a college campus, where the goal is liberal learning.

This does not mean that majors leading to specialized careers are inferior. However, it is important to examine how a major is taught. All should address three areas of concern: First, does it introduce students to the history and traditions of the discipline? Second, does it examine the social and economic implications? And finally, does it explore relevant ethical and moral issues? If these three criteria are met, the department offers an "enriched" major that not only encourages students to explore their field in depth, but also puts it into a larger perspective. It will teach necessary skills, but it will also require students to examine the history and implications of their discipline.

To cite some examples: Journalism students will learn how to write a news story, but they will also study the impact of information on society. Business majors may learn about marketing, but they will also understand their ethical responsibilities to customers. Within the sciences, students will explore the rich history of Western science and address the profound impact it has had on our lives.

How is this accomplished? Each major must offer a set of courses that puts the discipline in a larger perspective. An institution's course catalog will list the classes required in each major and deserves careful examination. How many focus on the development of technical "skills"? How many explore the broader understanding of the field?

General and Specialized Education Working Together

A strong general education program also helps enrich the major. For example, at Mount Saint Mary College, core classes continue into the sophomore year and beyond with additional seminars and courses exploring philosophy, theology, and ethics. In addition, students also study language, math, science, and social science. They move easily between general education and specialization during all years of study, carrying ideas from one to the other.

Northeastern University in Boston takes another approach that connects general education even more directly to the major. This university has rejected both a core curriculum and distribution requirements. Instead, general education and the major have been combined. All students at the university are required to learn essential skills, such as writing, speaking, and critical thinking. But how they learn is determined by their majors. For example, a business major will fulfill the requirement through courses that teach business communication. Meanwhile, an engineering student may meet the same goal through technical writing courses. The study of history, ethics, and culture—also required— will, likewise, be satisfied within the major. "We're trying to provide a common meaning for our students, but not give an identical program," says Amy Blodgett, who works in the office of the vice provost. "General education and the major are usually kept separate. We're trying to integrate general education *into* the major."

University administrators say students are the first to benefit. They see the relevance of general education to their study and are better able to apply what they have learned. Vague academic concepts become real and meaningful when, for example, a business student learns "communication skills" by writing a business plan or a nursing student comes to understand "diversity" by completing a practicum at an urban community health center. "It's not a situation where students in their freshman and sophomore year get general education thrown at them and don't have any context to put it in," says Michael Baer, Northeastern's provost for undergraduate education. "This is integrating the whole curriculum."

The program at Northeastern is experimental, but seems especially appropriate for institutions that emphasize professional degree programs. When looking at colleges and universities, investigate how they build bridges between specialized and general education.

A Concern for the Future

Most prospective college students do not know exactly what happens in college and cannot anticipate precisely how it will change their outlook on life. They may enter college searching for a career and financial security, but, along the way, discover many other rewards. The task is to find a college that lives up to all of these expectations. Although a good college or university works hard to excel in each of our ten categories, its commitment to a general education and an enriched major is one of the most important keys to quality. An institution that makes liberal learning an important part of every student's education is thinking not just how to attract students or help them get their first job after graduation. Instead, it is helping its students prepare for the future.

The Key Questions to Ask

Give special consideration to colleges that make general education an important part of the undergraduate curriculum. This is a clear sign that the college or university makes undergraduate education a priority.

1. Is general education a priority?
- Does the college or university offer a core curriculum (a sequence of required courses) or a carefully developed set of distribution requirements? If distribution requirements are used, students should pick from a limited list of classes that, preferably, have been created just for the general education program.
- How many general education courses are listed in the institution's course catalog? Do the courses appear connected to each other? Avoid colleges offering a long list of optional classes that are disconnected from each other and the rest of the curriculum.
- Does the institution limit how many credits students may take in the major?
- Does the institution discourage students from completing double majors?

2. Is general education supported through campuswide activities or off-campus travel?
- Are lectures, convocations, festivals, or other activities offered that directly support what is taught in the general education curriculum?
- Travel to museums, cultural events—or even other countries—extend general education into the community and around the world. What opportunities does the college or university offer students?

3. **Does the college or university offer an "enriched" major?**
   - Does each major, even the most specialized, examine its historical, social, and ethical implications?
   - Does general education support the major? For example, are required core courses taught during all years of study?

4

Finding the Best Teachers

Nothing matters more than the quality of teaching. It defines the college experience. When students describe what they like best about their schools, they almost always talk about their best professors. These are the teachers who made them feel welcome, inspired, and, in time, prepared for life.

Every college has at least a few truly exceptional teachers. These professors know a great deal about their discipline, of course, but they are loved by students because they go the extra mile. With an infectious enthusiasm, they make learning interesting and meaningful. They genuinely enjoy teaching and the company of students. But many colleges and universities also have less inspired teachers. In their hands, every subject becomes tedious and dry. In class, they are distracted and impatient; after class, they magically disappear. They seem to resent every minute spent with students.

Most common is the teacher who falls somewhere in between— ranging in most cases from good to adequate.

Students can easily tell the good from the bad and the best from all others. On every campus, there is an active student grapevine that compares the talents and failings of all faculty. At some universities, students have even published guides critiquing the teaching styles of instructors. Whether discussed informally around a dining hall table or published in a handbook, the message is clear: The quality of teaching on American colleges and universities varies greatly, and students, appropriately, want to learn from the best.

But is it possible to help students find the best teachers even before they enroll? Absolutely—by selecting a college that cares about teaching and helps good teachers become even better. By asking a few key questions, it is possible to find a college where good teaching is valued and rewarded.

Good Teachers Make the Difference

What do good teachers do? What makes them so special and their students so lucky?

More than anything else, exceptional faculty members care about their students. They like being around students, and they make them a priority. These faculty members are challenged—not frustrated—by the opportunity to educate undergraduates who have a great deal of enthusiasm but only limited knowledge. In addition, good teachers believe in a simple and honest way that education matters. They do more than "cover the material," they share a love of learning. These teachers are able to show how all knowledge is connected and how it is relevant to the lives of students.

The best teachers, in short, will be very much like John Trimble. A professor of English and writing at the University of Texas at Austin, he was recently honored by his colleagues for his ability as a teacher. A graduate of two prestigious universities—Princeton and Berkeley—he joined the faculty at Austin in 1970. Like most young professors, he taught a variety of undergraduate and graduate courses. But after several years, he dropped graduate teaching and dedicated his career to undergraduates. The reason is simple: he likes them better. "I think they're much more interesting," he explains. "They're enthusiastic. They don't have an attitude problem."

Equally important, he knows that these students need the attention and enthusiasm he can offer—especially when taking required English classes. "I like the idea of converting people, people who are not sure they want to write, not sure they like English," he says. "And unless they have a positive experience, they are apt to go out into the world thinking that English is not fun and writing and reading are not fun, and English professors are weird."

75

Treating Students Like People

After twenty-five years of experience, what are his strategies for success? First, he says, good teachers will be open and let students see them as real people, not just talking heads delivering lectures from a podium. He explains: "I give myself permission to be real, and I give myself permission to have fun. It's not that I'm jolly in the classroom, because frequently I'm very serious, but I don't try to be anything other than what I am. . . . Oddly enough, that's one of the hardest assignments for many [faculty members]: to be honest emotionally, intellectually, and, when we're ignorant, to 'fess up' freely without apology."

Equally important, he says, good teachers should get to know each of their students. In the classes he teaches, Trimble learns the students' names, majors, and interests. He also spends a great deal of time with students out of class. He is available for conferences in his office and at his home and gives students his home phone number—and encourages them to use it. "So I really do know my students," he concludes. "I care about them because the more I know them the better I can teach them and the less afraid of me they will be. They will feel known, understood, recognized, and appreciated."

Third, good teachers—in every discipline—will help students understand why they are learning. "I want my students to feel that what happens, what is talked about in class, is significant to their own lives." Can this be done in his field of English literature? Of course, he says. For example, when discussing classics of contemporary literature, such as *A Long Day's Journey into Night* or *The Iceman Cometh,* the class discussion may turn to the very relevant subject of an addiction—a theme of both books.

There are other requirements for good teaching. Faculty members must be experts in their fields who can also communicate information clearly. Too, they must have high academic expectations. Enthusiasm and concern has little meaning if it is not accompanied by skilled instruction.

However, it is clear that the best faculty members rely on more than well-organized lecture notes and carefully chosen textbooks. They show a dedication to teaching and a personal commitment to students. These faculty members not only make learning exciting, they change lives. They give confidence to uncertain scholars and wise counsel when career choices are being made. And, of greatest importance, they may become trusted friends who help younger students take the final steps into adult life and guide older students as they discover new talents.

Good teaching, then, is a complicated formula. No college or university has found a way to clone the John Trimbles. But they can—in their policies and values— encourage this kind of dedication.

In this chapter, we provide simple ways to discover if good teaching is a priority at the institutions you are considering. Most of the programs we describe happen "behind the scenes." Students usually do not see all the ways a college or university works to improve the quality of teaching. But they feel the results. Faculty members are attentive and enthusiastic in class and accessible after class. They work hard to make their courses better. When teaching is valued, students feel valued.

Who teaches?

A college that cares about teaching hires good teachers. Also, most undergraduate courses are taught by full-time faculty members, not graduate students or part-time instructors.

College and university viewbooks always talk about the dedication of their faculty, and most include pictures of professors working one-on-one with students. But how can an institution foster this kind of commitment? A meaningful first step is to make teaching ability an important criteria when hiring new faculty. Most faculty teach, but skill as an instructor is rarely given importance when new professors are being hired. Selection committees will scrutinize research and academic interests but give little attention to performance in the classroom.

Many colleges and a growing number of universities, however, are giving teaching ability more weight when making their selections. At these institutions, candidates are often asked to present a demonstration lecture or otherwise prove their ability and commitment to teaching. At Shorter College in Rome, Georgia, for example, candidates are required to present a sample lecture, which all students, faculty, and staff are invited to attend. Opinions of the candidate's teaching are collected and used when making the final decision.

This and similar efforts do not guarantee that every professor hired will excel in the classroom or will still be enthusiastic in ten years—especially if teaching is not supported in other ways. But it helps identify better teachers and, in time, can raise the quality of teaching within an institution. Most colleges do not talk to prospective students about how they select faculty. In recruitment literature, they may only talk about the faculty's "dedication" and "love of teaching." But it is worthwhile to ask admissions officers or current faculty how new faculty members are picked.

Evaluating the Role of Teaching Assistants

It is also useful to find out how many classes are taught by graduate students and part-time faculty, called adjuncts. At some institutions almost all introductory and lower division courses may be taught by teaching assistants—"T.A.s"—and part-timers.

It is important to stress that graduate students can be excellent teachers. Many are only a year or two away from finding work as full-time faculty and have a great deal of knowledge. Certainly, they have the expertise required to instruct introductory courses, and as young scholars, they are often enthusiastic about their subjects. Also, many teaching assistants are just that: assistants to professors. They do not teach their own classes but, instead, help the professor by grading papers and answering student questions. They may also lead smaller discussion classes, review sessions, or labs. In large lecture classes where hundreds of students are enrolled, they play an essential role.

Likewise, adjuncts have much to offer. Many are talented and qualified academics who have yet to find a permanent teaching position. The academic job market is very tight, creating a growing number of "gypsy scholars" who wander from one temporary appointment to another, sometimes for years.

Another group of part-time instructors are working professionals—such as journalists, business executives, and architects—who only teach one or two classes a semester. These people may be hired precisely because they can bring practical, real-world experience to students.

For example, City University in Renton, Washington, views its 900 adjuncts as an asset, not a liability. At this institution, most students are working professionals and most are pursuing professional degrees in business administration, accounting, marketing, and other career-oriented fields. In these disciplines, practical knowledge is valued, and college officials assert, students benefit when professors can teach from experience.

So a student who learns from a graduate student or adjunct is not necessarily getting cheated. It may be of concern, however, when the majority of classes are taught by these instructors. At some universities, it does suggest that undergraduate instruction is not taken seriously by administrators and senior faculty—T.A.s and adjuncts are given classes that full-time faculty would rather avoid.

In addition, when students depend on these instructors for much of their education, their weaknesses—even small ones—accumulate and become a liability. For example, graduate students are, as a group, the least experienced teachers, still learning how to manage a class and clearly present information. Part-timers may be less familiar with the university, and because most have other commitments—work in their profession or teaching at other colleges—they may be less accessible to students.

Parents are most concerned about the use of graduate students; many have heard horror stories about classes taught by T.A.s, especially those taught by foreign students who were not fluent in English. Some students complained they simply could not understand what these instructors were saying.

Embarrassed, many colleges and universities are working harder to screen and supervise their teaching assistants. At a minimum, many now test foreign T.A.s for their ability to speak English fluently. But some also make a conscientious effort to help their graduate students become good teachers.

Emory University in Atlanta, Georgia, has an especially aggressive program. There, every doctoral student is required to complete a special teacher training program. Students begin by learning how to write a course syllabus, grade assignments, give lectures, and lead discussions. When they first start working in the classroom, it is under the close supervision of a faculty member. Only after they have co-taught a course with a professor—and have met other academic requirements—are they allowed to apply for a teaching appointment.

Most faculty members are not formally trained in the art of teaching. They learn their craft by watching other teachers and through trial and error. The Emory program is part of a recent movement in America's universities to treat doctoral students as "student teachers," not just cheap teaching labor. They get the support and guidance any new teacher needs, which benefits both the T.A. and his or her students.

Many institutions have few or no teaching assistants. Four-year colleges, of course, do not have a pool of graduate students from which to draw. In addition, many universities are eager to explain that T.A.s have only a limited role on their campuses. For example, the College of William and Mary in Williamsburg, Virginia, offers graduate degrees but reports that only 1 percent of courses are taught by teaching assistants. At Ball State University in Muncie, Indiana, the figure is 3 percent. These institutions like to call themselves "teaching colleges" or "teaching universities," emphasizing their focus on instruction, not research.

Does this mean you should reject an institution that has more than a handful of teaching assistants? Not necessarily. Institutions that rely more heavily on graduate students may be the right fit. In addition, part-time instructors often bring real-world experience that students appreciate. But be wary if too many undergraduate classes are taught by graduate students and part-time instructors.

We propose that no more than 20 percent of faculty members should be part-time instructors and recommend that this figure also apply to graduate students. In other words, the majority of undergraduate classes should be taught by full-time faculty. The point is not that one kind of teacher is good and the others are bad. Rather, we believe there should be a healthy balance. If full-time faculty members are not able to teach all undergraduate classes, they should, at least, have a significant role, bringing their skills and special expertise to even introductory classes.

For example, at Old Dominion University in Norfolk, Virginia, all large lecture classes are taught by full-time faculty, not teaching assistants or adjuncts. "We think it's very important that freshmen get to see real faculty," explains Patricia Patten Cavender, vice president for enrollment services. "Public institutions are not well known for that anymore."

In addition, if teaching assistants and adjuncts are responsible for a large percentage of undergraduate teaching, be sure to ask how they are trained and supervised. If they don't have a well-organized program to mentor and oversee their teaching, we recommend you look elsewhere.

Is good teaching rewarded?

A college that values teaching recognizes good teachers. These institutions offer teaching awards and grant tenure only to those who can demonstrate excellence in the classroom.

For many professors, good teaching is its own reward. They don't need incentives to make students a priority. "What is truly amazing is that there are so many faculty in research universities who care about teaching despite the virtual absence of rewards for doing so," remarked one university task force quoted in *Change* magazine (July/August 1993).

But good teaching shouldn't have to be a heroic sacrifice. It should be respected and rewarded. "Nearly everyone, including the great majority of faculty at our most prestigious universities, agrees that teaching is undervalued and that the status of teaching should be elevated," writes

Russell Edgerton, president of the American Association for Higher Education, in the same issue of *Change*. He cites one survey of faculty from a respected state university system. It found that 97 percent of the faculty members polled believed that being a teacher was very important, but only 7 percent said faculty were rewarded for good teaching.

How can prospective students and parents tell if teaching matters at the colleges and universities they are considering? Begin by looking at how faculty get promoted and, especially, tenured. A college that cares about teaching will grant tenure only to faculty members who are skilled and attentive teachers.

Tenure Reveals an Institution's Priorities

Tenure is a mark of distinction in higher education. It brings greater job security and full acceptance as a scholar. But it doesn't happen automatically. Faculty members must satisfy often rigorous requirements and get the approval of their department and other special committees.

To gain tenure, most faculty members have to demonstrate excellence as both a scholar and a teacher. However, at many universities, the amount published is far more important than skill as a teacher. In fact, at some institutions, scholarship is all-important, and teaching has little influence in tenure decisions. For faculty at these institutions, the phrase "publish or perish" rings true.

More than any other single factor, tenure reveals the true priorities of a college or university. If good teaching has little or no value when tenure is being decided, this almost certainly reflects the status of teaching within the institution as a whole. So when looking at a college or university, be sure to ask how faculty members are evaluated. Although most institutions will say that teaching is considered—which is usually true—try to discover how much weight it actually carries. Does teaching have equal—or greater—value than research? Have faculty members been denied tenure because of poor teaching?

For example, Jacksonville State University in Jacksonville, Alabama, calls itself a "teach or perish" university. It—like other universities that focus on undergraduate instruction—considers the opinions of students when deciding tenure. It also says that sustained excellence in teaching must be demonstrated by faculty members who are candidates for promotion to full faculty.

Brescia College in Owensboro, Kentucky, reports that teaching has the highest priority in tenure and promotion decisions. Before tenure is granted, for example, students complete a special evaluation that becomes what one administrator calls a "critical part" of the faculty member's dossier. Likewise, the University of North Alabama in Florence says that teaching carries more weight than research or service.

Teaching Awards Support Good Instruction

Recently, a variety of colleges and universities have also started offering more public recognition of good teachers. At these institutions, one or more faculty receive a special teaching award each year. Top teachers are honored for their contributions and, often, are given a check—worth as much as $25,000—or even a permanent raise in pay.

These awards recognize teachers who have made students a priority. Until recently, most faculty members won acclaim only through their research. Teaching awards give long overdue attention to those who have dedicated themselves to the task of instruction. In addition, teaching awards are expected to improve the overall quality of teaching at that institution. They offer evidence to faculty that good teaching is valued and provide an incentive to make it a priority.

Transylvania University in Lexington, Kentucky, has an especially aggressive program to recognize good teachers. There, recognized faculty members are given between $8,000 and $12,000 annually for four years. Today, twenty-one faculty members hold this honor, reflecting about one third of all teachers at this small liberal arts college. The university also offers awards for new faculty members who are just being hired but show special promise as teachers. This one-time, $7,000 award helps recruit the best teachers, explains James Mosely, vice president and dean of the college. "It's especially difficult to find people who are coming out of graduate school who are then ready to teach at a liberal arts college. So we're trying to help people develop in that area."

At this college, the teaching award is a serious effort to honor the important work teachers do. It also raises the quality of teaching even higher in all classrooms. Mosely notes that the program "has had a significant impact on the campus culture." The outside review teams have brought new ideas to the campus, for example, and award recipients are expected to serve as mentors for new faculty.

Many other colleges and universities offer similar recognition. Drew University in Madison, New Jersey, provides a $10,000 prize for its distinguished teacher, which is awarded during graduation ceremonies. Boston University in Boston, Massachusetts, awards teaching prizes each year, both by the university and within each of the ten undergraduate colleges. At the College of William and Mary in Williamsburg, Virginia, three different teaching awards are offered, one each for new faculty, experienced faculty, and senior faculty.

Some in higher education worry that teaching awards are becoming little more than gimmicks and may not improve the quality of teaching. It has been noted, for example, that one annual award will have little impact at a large university where hundreds of faculty teach. Playing the odds, what is one instructor's chance of winning? And if there was little or no financial award, then the cynical professor might simply say, "Why bother?"

At other colleges, however, awards have great value and do help improve the quality of undergraduate instruction. How can parents and prospective students tell the difference? First, it never hurts to find out how much money is awarded. More money does not always equal greater prestige, but it can, especially if it means a permanent pay raise. A check for $5,000 is a welcomed gift, but a $5,000 raise can be a real incentive. Likewise, find out how many teaching awards are offered; educators assert awards are taken more seriously when a greater number are given. Most important, ask if teaching award recipients have any special responsibilities. For example, honored teachers at Transylvania University are expected to mentor new faculty. This suggests that its awards are not just beauty pageants, but part of a larger effort to improve instruction across campus.

Who teaches the teachers?

Good colleges help faculty become better teachers. They offer workshops, newsletters, and grants that help faculty learn about new teaching methods. They may also support a center for faculty development.

Colleges are now working to hire the best teachers and rewarding those who do it especially well. But a good college will do even more. It will also help faculty who want to become even better teachers. Today, many excellent colleges and universities encourage faculty members to continue their education as teachers. They provide seminars, study grants, and publications that introduce new teaching methods and help professors stay enthusiastic about their profession. Many even sponsor full-time offices, often called Centers for Teaching Excellence, where faculty can go for help and advice.

As a first step, faculty members are now given more opportunities to learn about new teaching methods. Many colleges and universities also help pay for the cost of attending conferences and developing new courses. For example, Kent State University in Kent, Ohio, has a travel program for faculty who want to attend conferences on teaching. There, faculty members can also get money to improve their own courses by, for example, writing computer programs or studying teaching methods at other universities. Likewise, Ohio Northern University in Ada, Ohio, offers Faculty Development Grants to instructors who are working to revise a course or want to attend a workshop on teaching.

These are relatively simple innovations. However, they reflect an important change in higher education. In the past, faculty members were given money and time needed to pursue research, but little or no support was given to improve the quality of teaching. These grants reflect a new understanding that teaching also deserves formal support. Do similar programs support faculty teaching at the institutions you are considering?

Helping Good Teachers Become Better

Many institutions also sponsor faculty development centers. These programs often have a permanent, full-time staff that offers workshops, newsletters, and support to individual faculty. On some campuses, these centers are especially active and help improve the quality of teaching all students receive. In the last three years, for example, the Faculty Development Center at Winona State University in Winona, Minnesota, has sponsored more than seventy workshops, lectures, video conferences, and colloquia. More than 200 faculty members—two thirds of the entire faculty—have taken part in these programs.

Workshops and seminars often focus on new teaching methods and, especially, the use of technology. Computers and video are having a dramatic influence on teaching. Many faculty members are making use of the Internet, e-mail, and interactive television as part of their courses. Although the chalkboard and overhead projector are not yet obsolete, they may be soon. Faculty need to know what is available and how it can be used effectively.

Of course, teaching can be improved in less dramatic ways. Seminars often ask professors to share simple tips for better teaching. At the University of Arkansas in Fayetteville, Arkansas, chemistry professor Wally Cordes has stressed to his colleagues the importance of knowing student names. But this is a difficult task when teaching a large lecture course. His solution? Take pictures. Cordes takes a Polaroid picture of each student, attaches the student's name, and commits it to memory. University officials report he is practically a campus celebrity for his ability to learn the names of all his students. But his point is important. He says the best way to provide individualized instruction is to know the individuals.

Looking Out for Poor Teaching

Faculty development centers help good teachers become better teachers. But, in some cases, their value is most dramatically confirmed when they confront genuinely poor teaching. At the University of Texas at Austin, Marilla

Sviniciki, director of the Center for Teaching Effectiveness, describes how she tried to help one instructor improve as a teacher but, in the end, recommended that he stay out of the classroom. "He was teaching a class that should have been very interesting. Even I could have made it interesting, and it wasn't my field," she says. "But I was bored to tears in that class. I couldn't believe it."

Talking to him later, she suggested ways to improve the class, but he dismissed all suggestions. "'Oh,' he said, 'that all takes so much time.'" So Sviniciki recommended that, if he couldn't make teaching a priority, he shouldn't teach at all. In the end, this instructor was fired by the university. This wasn't the place for him," she concludes. "He didn't like the undergraduates."

This story is unusual. Sviniciki stresses that most faculty members at her university show genuine interest in their students and, although they are pressured by multiple responsibilities, are able to give appropriate attention to their classes and students.

These programs will not change the quality of teaching overnight, but given time, it will improve. For example, the center at the University of Texas at Austin was started in 1973, and after nearly twenty-five years, its imprint is clear. "I think we've got a whole generation of new faculty who have gone [through these programs] and are doing a much better job in the classroom than those who go in cold," Sviniciki says.

How are teachers evaluated?

A good college regularly evaluates the quality of its faculty's teaching. Student opinions are collected in all classes and carefully considered. In addition, faculty members also review the teaching of their colleagues and mentor those needing help.

In nearly every profession, the quality of an employee's work is periodically reviewed. In the business world, especially, there is great interest in efficiency and productivity. Managers like to establish clear guidelines that employees must follow—how many widgets they should sell each month, how they should dress on the job—and then determine at regular intervals if workers measure up. In fact, there is a whole category of employees—called supervisors— who are given the job of looking over the shoulders of other employees.

Nothing like this exists in the academic world. This is not—as critics have argued for years—because academics are lazy and inefficient. Rather, it reflects respect for a different set of values. The currency of higher education is ideas, not money. Intellectual freedom, not corporate conformity, is most prized. For these reasons, the evaluation of faculty teaching is one of the hardest and most contentious issues in higher education. When educators start talking about the need to evaluate instructors, difficult questions must be asked: Can teaching ability be evaluated in a way that is fair and objective? Is it even possible to agree on what good teaching is? As John Trimble, the professor from Texas, made clear, good teaching is complex, personal, and not easily described.

Also, who will judge the quality of teaching? Faculty members have a great deal of autonomy, and many deeply resent the idea that others can come into their classes and pass judgment on the quality of teaching. Educators, however, acknowledge that faculty must somehow be accountable. If a college cannot establish some standards for classroom performance and ask all faculty to meet these requirements, then efforts to improve teaching will be incomplete. The task is slow and especially painful, but many agree it is necessary.

On every college and university campus, all faculty face some scrutiny, most often when tenure and promotions are being decided. For this, both teaching and research are usually evaluated. But the trend now is to look even more closely at teaching ability and to do it throughout a faculty member's full career.

Students benefit in two ways. First, it gives them a voice on campus; most colleges that review faculty performance use student evaluations, and the best colleges take their opinions seriously. In addition, it means that all faculty members are expected to make instruction a priority and to keep improving as a teacher. There is no opportunity to grow stale.

Faculty Members Should Evaluate Each Other

Student evaluations are the most common way to keep track of faculty. At a typical college or university, students are asked to fill out a form at the end of the semester offering their critiques of the class and instructor. These responses become part of the professor's file. They are also meant to be helpful to the instructor; weaknesses identified by students can be addressed.

But student opinion should be only one part of the evaluation process. There must also be regular review by other faculty members. This peer evaluation helps give a more complete picture of teaching skill. Also, faculty members who evaluate their colleagues are usually asked to do more than grade performance; they are expected to offer suggestions for improvement. This is important, of course, because evaluation is meaningless if it doesn't lead to better teaching.

At the Farquhar Center for Undergraduate Studies at Nova Southeastern University in Fort Lauderdale, Florida, for example, faculty members are evaluated regularly by students and other teachers. According to Dean Stuart Horn, students complete evaluation forms for every class and every instructor. These forms are reviewed by the department chair and discussed with faculty. They are saved and used again for later comprehensive reviews. New faculty members are also evaluated by their peers every year, and even the most senior faculty members are evaluated every three years. For these reviews, colleagues visit classes and then write a report summarizing student comments. Faculty members also submit a self-evaluation, where they assess their relationships with students, community service, and other work.

Faculty members who need to strengthen their teaching skills develop a specific plan for improvement. Other teachers come together as a team to help and work during the whole year to make necessary changes. "The team will then meet at the end of the year and examine whether or not there has been progress," says Horn. He stresses that the process is supportive, not threatening. "We see this not as an adversarial situation. It's not like, 'Either you do this or you're out.'" But it is also understood that improvements will be made.

In at least one institution, students are also asked to take part in this process. At Belmont University in Nashville, Tennessee, some faculty members encourage their students to offer suggestions during the semester—not just at the end. Students meet weekly or biweekly with professors to discuss how classes are going and to make specific suggestions for improvement. So if a professor is not presenting material clearly or has poor rapport with students, the conferences can lead to immediate changes.

Few colleges have this level of student participation. But at the best colleges and universities, all faculty members are evaluated by students and other teachers. These evaluations are taken seriously by faculty and administrators; they determine whether or not tenure and promotions are given.

Evaluations, however, are one part of a more comprehensive effort to improve the quality of teaching. A good college or university emphasizes teaching skill when new faculty members are being hired and make sure that even the most senior faculty members have a commitment to teaching. They also provide opportunities for professional growth and reward those who excel. Teaching, after all, is the first role of the faculty in American higher education, and undergraduate students are the foundation of most institutions. The president of Duke University, in Durham, North Carolina, Nannerl O. Keohane, reminded his colleagues in the fall 1993 issue of *Daedalus* that "Undergraduates, and their parents, support our enterprise with their tuition and fees. . . . By accepting the support they give us, we enter into a bargain with those students and their families. We have an obligation to uphold our end of it." Professor John Trimble makes a similar point in more personal terms. "Students are my meal ticket," he notes. "If I didn't have them, I wouldn't have a job."

These simple observations, when taken to heart, help build institutions where undergraduate students are at the center, not the fringes, of college life. But when a college or university takes the opposite path and neglects the teaching role, students begin to feel like extras in a movie production. They fill space but know that the real action is directed elsewhere.

The good news is that most faculty members do, in fact, care deeply about students and their role as teachers and mentors. In addition, many institutions are offering the programs and incentives that reestablish an appropriate balance between teaching and other academic roles. Many other colleges have never abandoned their original commitment to students and teaching. By asking a few questions and listening closely to the answers given, it is not hard to find a college where students are given the attention and support they deserve from the people who matter most—their teachers.

The Key Questions to Ask

Within every college or university, the quality of teaching varies. But it is possible to identify institutions that try to support good teaching and make good teachers even better.

1. Who teaches?
- Is teaching skill evaluated when new faculty members are hired? For example, are candidates asked to teach a class or otherwise prove their skill in the classroom?
- Are undergraduate classes taught primarily by full-time faculty?
- Are teaching assistants formally trained and supervised as they learn the art of instruction?

2. Is good teaching rewarded?
- Is teaching ability seriously evaluated when tenure is being decided? Have faculty members been denied tenure for poor teaching ability?
- Are annual teaching awards given? How many? Is there a monetary award?

3. Who teaches the teachers?
- Are faculty members who receive teaching awards expected to mentor other faculty?
- Are grants available to faculty members who wish to develop new courses or learn about new teaching methods?

- Does the college or university support a center for instructional improvement?

4. **How are teachers evaluated?**
   - Are students asked to evaluate every class?
   - Are these evaluations considered for tenure and promotion?
   - Are faculty members also expected to evaluate teaching performances of their colleagues—and help make improvements?
   - Does this peer review continue throughout a professor's full career?

5

The Creative Classroom

The typical college class is still a room filled with rows of seated students. A lecture is delivered, perhaps a few questions are answered. Then notebooks are closed and everyone leaves. But many courses are now being dramatically reorganized. Students can take part in lively discussions, work together, and share responsibility for assignments. Also, learning does not always take place in a classroom: fieldwork and research projects enrich the college experience. The most innovative colleges and universities encourage their students to learn in many different ways, with a focus on active learning. This means that students are not just passive recipients of information. Instead, they learn by doing and participate in their own education.

These changes help bring learning to life. Students can share opinions, work side-by-side with a professor on research, or extend the classroom into the surrounding community. For them, knowledge exists everywhere, not just on a chalkboard or in a textbook.

This kind of creative activity is gaining favor among educators because it works. Students get more out of college, and they are better prepared to succeed after graduation. There is another advantage: Competition between students for top grades is often replaced by an atmosphere of cooperation, providing an environment for learning that is more supportive and less threatening. Of course, lectures have a role to play, but they are not the only way to learn. A good college will be a place where the classes are not limited to a room with four walls and where faculty members make students their partners.

In the last chapter, we described how colleges and universities can support good teachers. In this chapter, we show how these teachers put their skill and dedication to use in the classroom. We explain how you can recognize an institution that makes active learning a priority.

Education as a Human Enterprise

American colleges—and large universities most of all—have become experts in crowd control. A visit to any large institution on a registration day reveals how higher education is, indeed, a learning industry.

Students queue in one line after another, waiting for their turn with a registrar, cashier, adviser, or bookstore clerk. Progress is tracked, with mechanical precision, on computers. Social security numbers—not names or academic interests—are students' first form of identification. Standing amid this organized chaos, it is easy to forget that learning is, above all, a human enterprise. Ultimately, success is defined not by the efficient movement of bodies in and out of the institution. Instead, it depends on the ability to reach out to each student, individually, and make them active partners in their own education.

Too often, however, the assembly line continues into the classroom. Lecture classes—sometimes holding hundreds of students—define much of undergraduate education. In the largest classes, students may arrive and leave unknown to their professors.

There is, however, evidence of change on campuses across the country. Colleges and universities are reorganizing their classrooms and, occasionally, their entire curricula to allow new styles of learning and to put the focus back on students. Faculty and administrators talk about "active learning." One influential 1987 report from the Johnson Foundation (*Seven Principles for Good Practice in Undergraduate Education*) explained the approach this way:

> Learning is not a spectator sport. Students do not learn much just sitting in classes listening to

teachers, memorizing prepackaged assignments, and spitting out answers. They must talk about what they are learning, write about it, relate it to past experience, and apply it to their daily lives. They must make what they learn part of themselves.

In this chapter, we feature colleges and universities that foster this kind of learning. At these institutions, students are able to work closely with faculty and other students. Walk into a classroom and you will not see a formal lecture, but a conversation: questions are asked, answered, challenged—and respectfully discussed—by all. Students may even be working in groups, sharing ideas and responsibility for assignments. Or, perhaps, students have left the classroom; individually or as a class, they will be found, instead, completing research in a laboratory, community, or even another country.

If active learning is supported across campus, students can step off the educational assembly line. Each classroom becomes its own small, nurturing community where students have a voice and an opportunity to contribute.

Do teachers know their students?

Active learning rarely takes place in a large lecture class. Instead, a college committed to more student participation must, as a first step, offer small classes and opportunities for out-of-class interaction with faculty.

Most of the programs we feature in this chapter have one thing in common: Students are working closely, and often individually, with faculty. There is rapport between students and teachers, and the classroom becomes a true community.

This is a fundamental first requirement for learning in the creative classroom, but it can only happen in small classes and small groups.

So when evaluating the quality of instruction, look first at the size of classes being taught. A college that values active learning must offer more small classes, even in introductory freshman courses. When large lecture courses are necessary, they will be supplemented by small discussion sections.

Class size is a simple indicator of quality, but it is not always easy to evaluate. Recruitment literature from most colleges and universities—even the largest state institutions—often gives the impression that every student gets personal attention. If viewbooks reflected reality, then no class in American higher education enrolls more than a dozen students, and most classes are held outside on warm spring days.

Looking Beyond Student-Faculty Ratios

Most prospective students and their parents are justifiably skeptical of this literature. But they do pay attention to what appears to be a more reliable indicator: student-faculty ratios. The ratio of students to teachers is often reported by colleges. The assumption is that institutions with a lower ratio offer smaller classes and can give more attention to each student.

But these numbers do not tell the whole story. A 12:1 ratio may sound good, but because this number is an average, it does not reveal the full range of class sizes. Although many juniors and seniors may enjoy small classes at this institution, required freshman and sophomore courses could still enroll hundreds of students. Further, the college or university may be counting nonteaching faculty, such as full-time researchers or instructors who are on leave.

Ratios are not enough to make an informed choice. When judging class sizes, it is important to investigate the institution more thoroughly. For example, find out not just the average class size, but the size of the largest classes taken by undergraduates. Especially, find out the size of the largest general education classes. These are the courses that are most often overloaded. The admissions office should have these figures, if they are not reported in recruitment literature.

Many colleges can tell you more. For example, Denison University in Granville, Ohio, reports that 80 percent of classes have fewer than twenty-five students and a quarter of classes have fewer than ten students. At Marlboro College in Marlboro, Vermont, 94 percent of classes have fewer than twenty students, and 60 percent have fewer than ten.

Liberal arts colleges and small universities, it must be acknowledged, typically offer more small classes; large lecture classes so common at many research universities usually don't even exist. This is one of the distinct advantages of small institutions. But, increasingly, even some of the largest universities are making a deliberate effort to give their students more personal attention and opportunities to study in smaller classes. Some colleges—both large and small—offer a variety of unique programs that allow faculty and students a chance to work together in different ways.

Discussion Groups Encourage More Interaction

Universities cannot afford to tear down their lecture halls. But some are supplementing large classes with small discussion groups. For example, Pace University, which enrolls more than 12,000 students in New York City, includes discussion sections with some of its biology, history, math, and chemistry courses. Groups of just eight to ten students meet regularly with a student mentor who can help answer questions and talk informally about ideas presented in class. These seminars offer what a large class cannot—casual conversation and support from other students.

The University of Missouri–Rolla has a similar program for students enrolled in what it calls "make-or-break" freshman physics, chemistry, and calculus courses. Its group learning workshops are held three times a week and are also led by student mentors. Participation is voluntary, but university officials report nearly all freshmen take part. Those who do are also more likely to stay enrolled and get better grades.

Spending Time with Faculty Outside the Classroom

Colleges and universities of all sizes also recognize the importance of out-of-class interaction with teachers. Time spent talking in the office, home, or dormitory is often the most meaningful for students. Some of the most important opportunities for intellectual growth exist between classes, when students can engage their teacher one-on-one. These meetings can turn faculty into mentors and even friends.

This happens naturally at many colleges. However, ask if the college or university works deliberately to encourage interaction between students and faculty. Williams College in Williamstown, Massachusetts, for example, helps pay for the expense of entertaining students in faculty homes. As another enticement, faculty and students also receive free food and drink when they meet together in the college snack bar.

Other colleges take a different approach. A few have adopted a unique calendar where students take just one course at a time. The Colorado College in Colorado Springs has divided its academic year into eight three-and-a-half week segments, with each block devoted to a single class. Since students and professors are not distracted by other obligations, they can devote full attention to the class and to each other. Professors have even held classes off campus for a day or even the whole month.

These programs are diverse, but they have a common goal. Each is trying to build connections between teachers and students, both in and out of the classroom. This can be accomplished, first, by offering small classes. In addition, the relationship that is built in class can be extended in small group discussions and informal seminars. Finally, a college of quality will encourage students and teachers to spend time together out of class.

Do students participate in class?

In the creative classroom, students play a bigger role. Courses may be organized as seminars where faculty members guide lively student discussions. Teachers may also encourage students to work cooperatively on assignments. In some cases, students may even become teachers.

It is not enough to know that a college offers small classes. You should also examine how classes are taught. Small classes are most important because they allow faculty to teach in more flexible and innovative ways. With small classes and greater individual attention from teachers, students can contribute more in the classroom. There is no back row in these classes; faculty members encourage student participation and, in some cases, expect students to help direct the class.

How is this kind of participation encouraged? First, classes are taught as seminars, where students actively discuss and debate issues. In these courses, faculty members do not lecture; they guide discussions and encourage all students to take part. The teacher leads by posing questions and highlighting key points; the class has the energy and informality of a conversation.

All colleges and universities offer at least some seminar-style classes, but at a good college, this kind of learning is available to all students, even during the freshman year. At Coker College in Hartsville, South Carolina, for example, nearly all courses are taught as seminars during all years of study. No class has more than twenty students, and students and teachers also sit together at specially designed round tables, an arrangement that encourages conversation. Only science classes that include laboratory work are taught in classrooms with traditional desks and tables.

"The round table approach is active learning involving the whole class as a team," says Frank Bush, executive vice president of the college. "Students not only learn their subject matter, they also learn how to think critically and creatively and to express themselves in front of others." Bush says new students may be intimidated by this unusual classroom arrangement—there is no place to hide when sitting at a round table. But students quickly discover its benefits. When students are expected to contribute in each class, they soon become confident and articulate learners. "The change we see in our freshmen to seniors in unbelievable," he says.

If you have an opportunity to visit a college and can attend classes, examine how they are taught. Are students contributing to the content of each class? Are they interacting with each other, or just with the instructors? Are faculty members able to generate lively conversations that include most students? Do students come to class prepared for discussion? Is the mood of each class civil and respectful?

As you walk around campus, also note how desks are arranged in the classrooms. Rows of desks facing a podium suggest that classes held in this room rely on faculty lectures. If the desks are bolted to the floor, then any other kind of learning becomes almost impossible. But if chairs are arranged less formally—in a circle or semicircle—then student participation is more likely.

Encouraging Students to Work Together

The opportunity for discussion is the first benefit of small classes. But creative teachers may also ask their students to learn in other ways. Students may also collaborate on assignments and special projects, sharing ideas and responsibility for the final product.

At Clarkson University in Potsdam, New York, for example, engineering students have worked in teams to construct a solar-powered car and an all-terrain vehicle for design competitions. On the West Coast, engineering students at California State University at Chico have worked together to design a hybrid electric vehicle. Construction management students at this school recently won a design competition with their plan of a fourteen-story building for downtown San Francisco. Sara Armstrong, vice provost for academic affairs, says the design was completed in just 24 hours and was surprisingly close to the final rendering that professional architects developed for the actual building.

Such competitions are popular in many professional programs. Students in engineering, architecture, and computer science are being given more opportunities to solve real-work design problems. But many other disciplines are also involved in creative group projects.

At Fairfield University in Fairfield, Connecticut, business students have worked in teams to learn management and marketing skills by building an eleven-foot-long model airplane. In this semester-long exercise, each group developed a plan for financing and marketing the project. They also had to hire and train a "pilot" to guide its flight. Some groups even divided construction responsibilities among subcontractors. Always they had to keep an eye on the bottom line. "They had to go through the planning of how you put together a firm that does some assembly work," says Associate Dean Walter Ryba. Like the real world, the product had to work. "To pass the course, their airplane had to actually fly," he adds.

Other programs have been inspired by television game shows. Accounting students at Widener University in Chester, Pennsylvania, test their knowledge by competing in teams modeled after *Jeopardy*. The university even hosted an intercollegiate Accounting Jeopardy competition. At Susquehanna University in Selinsgrove, Pennsylvania, biology professor Jack Holt tests his students by playing a modified version of *Jeopardy*, rather than traditional tests or quizzes.

Team learning is growing in popularity, and research confirms its value. "Students learn better through noncompetitive collaborative group work than in classrooms that are highly individualized and competitive," according to Kenneth Bruffee, director of the Scholars Program at Brooklyn College. In addition, this kind of learning mirrors the real world, where most work requires cooperation with peers.

Every college has a few teachers who display this kind of creativity in the classroom. But look for evidence that collaboration is encouraged across the institution. Is group work a formal part of some—or all—majors? Does the college or university train and support faculty members who want to include teamwork in their classrooms? The best schools actively encourage this kind of learning.

Students Should Also Be Teachers

Finally, students are not only participating in classes, they are also being asked to help teach classes. Working under close supervision from faculty, a growing number of colleges and universities are discovering that undergraduates can be excellent instructors. In some cases, they lead discussions or answer questions, acting as mentors and tutors to their peers. Occasionally, they also help design and run whole courses.

Massachusetts Institute of Technology (MIT) in Cambridge, for example, is proud of its distinguished faculty, which include Nobel laureates. But administrators also talk with enthusiasm about their use of undergraduates as teachers. In an alternative first-year program called the Experimental Study Group, about one quarter of the teaching faculty members are undergraduate students. Students admitted into this selective program take most of their first-year courses in classes so small that the largest enrollment is four. The average class size is three. "That's instead of a lecture with 300 hundred students," notes program coordinator Holly Sweet.

But what makes the program even more unusual is its diverse faculty. Teachers include top researchers and retired faculty. But some are current students who have been through the program. The combination seems incongruous, but administrators insist that undergraduates make excellent teachers and can, in fact, bring some unique skills into the classroom. "They become like big brothers and sisters," says Sweet. "They can talk to [fellow students] at a level they can understand. . . . They're not condescending, and they are really accessible."

In this and other colleges, administrators acknowledge that undergraduate teachers are economical. At MIT, for example, Holly Sweet says her program could not maintain its extraordinarily low teacher-student ratio without the use of student teachers. But the advantages are not just financial. When undergraduate students are allowed to become teachers, they are also gaining leadership skills essential in any profession. In addition, when the teaching role is shared, learning becomes richer and more dynamic—the classroom becomes a far more interesting place.

When evaluating colleges, ask if undergraduates are ever expected to assume the role of teacher in courses, lab sections, or small discussion groups. Then ask: How extensive is the program? How are they trained and supervised? You may find a college that gives its students a chance to discover knowledge in exciting new ways.

Each of these programs rejects the traditional college classroom. Instead of seeing the teacher as the conduit of all knowledge, the creative classroom draws on the expertise of students. By learning together, working collaboratively, and, when appropriate, assuming leadership roles, students take responsibility for their education.

Does learning take place outside of the classroom?

Learning does not only occur in classrooms. Innovative colleges extend the campus into the surrounding community and even abroad. Fieldwork and foreign travel can be made a formal part of many classes. Computers can bring the world back into even the most isolated classroom.

At many colleges and universities, the boundaries between the classroom and community are falling away. They now encourage, and sometimes even require, students to earn credit for work and travel off campus. More than a field trip to a museum, entire courses may now take place away from the classroom. Other colleges use telecommunications, allowing students to travel electronically to resources and people across the nation and around the globe.

These experiences, when carefully organized and supervised by faculty, can be the most meaningful part of a student's education. They allow students to discover knowledge and apply what they have learned in ways that cannot be duplicated in any traditional classroom. It is the ultimate form of active learning.

Elon College in Elon College, North Carolina, reports that it recently redesigned its curriculum and revamped more than 700 courses to put greater emphasis on learning beyond the classroom. There, all students are now required to take part in fieldwork by, for example, completing internships or studying abroad. Also, many classes now take students out into the community where they have become advocates for social and environmental issues.

For example, one class studied the region's social needs, and another helped save a family homestead from being turned into a landfill. A philosophy course also requires students to complete a service project to show that "philosophy is not just a mind game," says Clair Myers, dean of arts and sciences. Some students have met this requirement by working with residents at a senior citizens home.

At this college and other institutions that emphasize real-world experience, students are asked to think about what they have learned through journals and papers. "All of these projects require some sort of reflection so the experience doesn't hang out here on the side but is indeed centered in the learning," says Myers.

When looking at colleges and universities, find out if opportunities for off-campus learning exist. Also ask how students are helped to make these experiences a meaningful part of their academic studies. How are they guided and advised during their work? How are they expected to use the knowledge they gained back on the campus and in their classes?

Making the World Your Classroom

Some colleges and universities have made a special commitment to international education. At Drew University in Madison, New Jersey, about one third of the sophomore class participates in a year-long international seminar. As part of this program, students travel with faculty, in small groups, on four-week study trips to different sites around the world. Students in this program are more than tourists; they are expected to complete an on-site research project, which is completed and analyzed after their return, according to dean Paolo Cucchi.

But a growing number of students are now able to travel abroad without leaving the classroom. At some colleges, classes use telecommunications to carry on conversations with students in other countries. Ramapo College in Mahwah, New Jersey, has made videoconferences and audioconferences a significant part of its curriculum for a decade. Students studying international politics, environmental issues, foreign languages, and other subjects take part in seminars with faculty and students in such countries as Russia, China, and Italy through teleconferences.

Such international conversations are a regular part of the curriculum, says President Robert Scott. For example, a course in international politics is formally linked to a similar class offered at a Russian university. "They use teleconferencing to discuss the course materials as well as contemporary issues," he says. While this technology does not replace actual travel and study abroad, it can enrich the content of almost any class. "We can take our students, for a class period, into another country," Scott says.

111

Teleconferences are a special feature of Ramapo College, and more than half of the faculty members have made it some part of their classes. A quality education does not require this kind of technology, but a college that does incorporate telecommunication into the classroom—and does it well—is offering another way to reach beyond the classroom.

Do students take part in research?

A good college or university will encourage students to conduct real research. They will have opportunities to work alongside faculty, completing experiments in the laboratory or discovering new information in the library or field. Students will also be asked to complete their own original research.

At most universities and many colleges, research is a major part of faculty work. Professors spend many hours in laboratories and libraries, completing scholarship for publication. Most of this work, however, has been off-limits to undergraduates, who, it was assumed, were too inexperienced to complete their own original research or assist faculty.

Many educators have changed their minds. One of the most exciting movements in higher education is to bring these students into the community of scholars and make them partners in the research process. Increasingly, they are completing their own research, presenting papers at professional conferences, and working one-on-one with scientists on serious investigations. In this way, students can actually benefit from faculty research, and a strong research role can be an asset, not a liability, for undergraduates.

Colleges and universities around the country are making undergraduates their research partners. At Spelman College, a historically black college for women in Atlanta, Georgia, most students take part in some kind of original research before graduation. According to Provost Glenda Price, they may help conduct experiments in a lab. Other students are actually paid through the college's work-study program to assist faculty members with their research. For example, one foreign language student was hired to conduct phone interviews with Latin American artists for a faculty member's book. Students can also travel during the summer to research universities around the country for internships.

"We think that undergraduate research is critical. We try to the degree we can to have every student, at some time, participate in some kind of research with us," Price says. All students in the sciences take part in research, and overall, 60 percent of the entire student body leaves with some experience in original research.

Many large state universities have similar opportunities for undergraduate students. The University of North Carolina at Greensboro and the California State University, Fullerton, both report that undergraduates may work as partners with faculty on meaningful research. Many other institutions have some kind of program that allows similar work.

It is important to investigate, however, what role students play in the lab. Too often they are given only minor tasks—washing test tubes—while the real work goes on without their participation. In these cases, students are completing what Glenda Price from Spelman calls "scutwork that the faculty member doesn't want to pay somebody to do." "While there is some value to just being in the environment where research is taking place, it's important that they actually do the real research," she adds. Look, then, for programs where students are actually conducting experiments and collaborating on studies.

Learning Science by Doing Science

Colleges and universities are also changing how they teach research skills. Many now ask first-year students to become scholars by practicing scholarship. For example, some institutions are rebuilding their science courses, allowing students to learn biology, chemistry, and other subjects by completing true experiments. Students are asked to propose research questions, design experiments, and report the results even in introductory courses.

The State University of New York at Binghamton offers several courses where freshmen devise experiments in the laboratory. Although they are carefully guided by faculty and more experienced student mentors, students in the first semester of college will learn science by practicing science. Students enrolled in "Introduction to Biology" have experimented with an enzyme that makes fruit turn brown. Working in groups, students have examined this enzyme in different fruits, looked for ways to prevent browning, or examined the characteristics of the enzyme. Although these experiments do not lead to startling new discoveries, they do follow the scientific method, and their investigations provide all of the excitement, and frustration, of work done by professionals.

This program is unlike traditional introductory science courses. While most traditional courses include laboratory work, students are usually not asked to design their own experiments. Rather, they complete prescribed lab work that, if done correctly, leads to predicted results. Everyone is completing the same work and ends up at the same place.

Why have a program that is so much more time-consuming? According to Anna Tan Wilson, who coordinates the project and is a member of the biological sciences faculty, the focus on research allows students to see what science is all about. "It's extremely difficult to get science across to students unless you do it this way," she says. It is also a better way to learn, she adds. "We really believe students learn a lot by doing. It is not just a question of knowing the vocabulary and understanding all the concepts. They're here to be trained as scientists, and therefore, we're going to give them the whole experience right from the very beginning."

The program at SUNY Binghamton is a significant part of the science curriculum. Every semester, as many as 400 students take the "Introduction to Biology" class. In addition, four other upper division biology courses follow a similar hands-on approach to research.

Research in the Humanities

Research is also a part of the humanities. Scholars in history, philosophy, and English also work to discover new knowledge and propose new theories. Here, too, undergraduates are taking part. Exemplary colleges and universities expect students to work with original sources and data. Many now also require students to write a major paper before graduation.

Reed College in Portland, Oregon, is one of a growing number of colleges that require all students to complete a senior thesis—a major research paper—as a graduation requirement. This year-long project requires students to make use of all the writing and critical thinking skills they have learned in college and demonstrate—just like their colleagues in graduate school—an area of special expertise.

Is service learning part of the curriculum?

A good college asks all students to complete a project that benefits a community or helps those in need.

Service has been a consistent theme in this book because we are convinced that education is not simply a path to personal opportunity, but a tool for social renewal. Knowledge and skills learned in college can, and should, help build a stronger nation at a time when it seems consumed by so much anger and division. Every college should encourage this kind of contribution, and a growing number of colleges do. Many incorporate service learning into specific courses, while others sponsor offices that help place students into the community. At some schools, this work is voluntary; at others it is required for graduation.

What kind of work do students complete? At Santa Clara University in Santa Clara, California, students work in a homeless shelter, a senior center, and help teach English as a second language to adult students. Calvin College in Grand Rapids, Michigan, has a service-learning center that places students with needy children in day-care centers, at food banks, and with environmental organizations. Many campuses also work with Habitat for Humanity, a nonprofit organization that helps build low-cost housing.

The list is almost endless, reflecting the needs of each community. But in each case, these programs build understanding and show that individuals can make a difference. No less important, students often say that, in the end, they were the ones who gained the most.

At a minimum, a college or university should provide a clearinghouse for students searching for service-learning opportunities. Ideally, this will be a requirement for graduation and formally incorporated into the curriculum.

Finally, some kind words for the much-maligned lecture hall. Most students attend mid- to large-size universities; most of these schools offer lecture classes, many filled with hundreds of students. Is this bad?

We believe education is made richer when students work with faculty members and with each other. This kind of learning should be available to all students, even freshmen, at all institutions.

But, without question, there is also a place for large-scale learning. For example, convocations may bring a department—or a whole school—together into an auditorium, helping to build a stronger sense of community and common purpose. In addition, some classes fill large lecture halls because student demand is so great. To give just one example, Vincent Scully of Yale University has for thirty years delivered lectures that attract 500 or more students at a time. Although his subject happens to be architecture, his skill and insight draw students from all disciplines. Many say his classes were the most memorable part of their education, according to Lee Mitgang, author of a new report on architecture education. Certainly, here—and everywhere—learning of the highest order can be found.

So we are not proposing that you avoid lectures at all costs (which would be impossible at most institutions). Rather, look for a healthy balance. The creative classroom comes in many shapes and sizes.

The Key Questions to Ask

Do the colleges and universities you are considering make active learning a priority?

1. **Do teachers know their students?**
   - What are the average undergraduate class size?
   - What is the largest and the smallest classes taught?
   - Specifically, how big is the largest required general education class?
   - If large lecture classes are offered, are they accompanied by small discussion sections?
   - How does the institution encourage informal interaction among faculty and students?

2. Do students participate in class?

- Are first-year and introductory classes taught as seminars where students carry on discussions?
- Do students regularly work in small groups? Are they encouraged to collaborate on assignments and special projects? Is this a formal part of degree programs?
- Do students have the opportunity to become mentors, or even teachers, to other students? How extensive is the program? How are the students trained and supervised?

3. Does learning take place outside the classroom?

- What opportunities exist for off-campus learning?
- What percentage of students earn credit for work completed off campus?
- How are students guided and advised as they complete off-campus studies?
- Are telecommunications and other forms of electronic learning incorporated into classroom instruction? How many professors use this technology? Are they formally trained in its proper use?

4. Do students take part in research?

- Are there opportunities for undergraduates to take part in faculty research? What role do they play? What percentage of students assist with faculty research?
- Are all students expected to complete their own original research—such as a senior thesis—before graduation?

5. Is service learning part of the curriculum?

- Do students earn credit for volunteer work?
- What percentage of students participate in service learning?

6

Resources for Learning

"How many books are in the library?" This is often the first question asked when evaluating what educators like to call the "heart of every college." But the answer varies dramatically—50,000 volumes at one college, 5 million at another university. How many are enough? Is this the only key to quality?

With their stately architecture and large collections, libraries offer proof that an institution is truly a center of knowledge. But appearances can be deceptive. What matters most is not the library's size. Instead, the quality of its collection and, especially, the commitment of its staff to the education of students is the true mark of a good library. At the best colleges and universities, the library is far more than a collection of books and periodicals. It also plays an active role in the education of students, helping them become savvy consumers of information. Graduates from these institutions are prepared to be lifelong learners because they know how to expertly find—and use—knowledge.

These libraries also help sustain what is often called the "culture of the book." They sponsor readings and other special events that honor literature and encourage students to make reading a habit. Although modern libraries are on the cutting edge of new information technology, they are also grounded in an ancient tradition that respects books and everything they symbolize: wisdom, reflection, and entertainment. A library can help preserve and celebrate this heritage.

Further, a library is no longer limited by the size of its own collection. Computer technology now allows electronic access to journal articles and even entire books located at institutions across town and around the world. Today, the ability to gain access to this information is no less important than the size of a library's own collection.

The Empty Library

Every college and university has a library, and many are housed in impressive buildings. But what would happen if, one day, the library—all its books and staff—suddenly disappeared? At the best institutions, learning would grind to a halt. Students would lose a vital resource needed to complete assignments and original research. Faculty would lose the support and expertise of librarians who help shape the curriculum. But at too many institutions, very little would change. Students, faculty, and administrators might barely notice the loss. Classes would go on as scheduled; assignments would be completed without delay.

Although the library is, indeed, universally praised as an essential part of higher education, many educators have observed a gap between rhetoric and reality. In 1959, Patricia Knapp noted pessimistically in her book *College Teaching and the College Library* that "most students use the library very little, [and] some students manage to do adequate college work without using it at all." More recently, another librarian echoed this concern. "The fact is that academic libraries touch too few lives," writes Robert K. Baker in a 1995 issue of the journal *College & Research Libraries*.

Does this mean the college library is less important than many believe? Hardly. Instead, it reflects a long-standing concern in higher education that libraries are not put to good use by educators. Faculty assign textbooks but may not expect students to find information on their own. "They are not requiring their students to independently find, use, and evaluate information as an integral (and graded) component of the courses they teach," Baker continues.

A poorly used library is, then, an indictment not of students, but of the whole institution. Teachers are not challenging their students to explore new knowledge and develop skills they will use for the rest of their lives. If students can succeed without even walking into a library—or using it only as a quiet place to read—it means they are not being asked to think deeply about the subjects they study. The library can suffer in other ways. When money is tight, library budgets are often among the first to be cut. The collection then cannot keep pace with the explosive growth of new information or changes in the curriculum. Also, fewer professional librarians may be on staff—and work fewer hours—which may make the library less user friendly and even less relevant.

A tour of a university library may reveal many rows of neatly shelved books, periodicals, and indexes—but few people using its resources. It might be book rich, but people poor.

The library should be seen as an important resource and deserves careful scrutiny during your college selection process. In this chapter, we describe the qualities of a good academic library and explain how you can confidently identify a college that serves the information needs of students.

Answers to the questions that follow in this chapter will tell you a great deal about the strength of the library and offer insight into the intellectual health of the whole institution. If library resources are actively used and its staff members are respected as members of the faculty, this may be evidence that the college or university shares a true love of learning. But if the library sits apart—largely irrelevant to faculty, students, and the curriculum—then it has become more like a museum. Information is stored for posterity, not for real use, possibly revealing a deeper malaise throughout the whole institution.

Does the library's collection serve the needs of undergraduate students?

What matters most is not the total number of books and journals held in the library, but rather, how well this collection serves the needs of undergraduate students. If the holdings are outdated or more attentive to the interests of faculty and graduate students, even the largest library will be a frustration.

All libraries contain a great deal of information. But, for prospective students, the important question is this: Do they hold the right kind of information?

Every library must maintain a core collection of books, periodicals, and other resources most useful for undergraduate students. The Carnegie Foundation report, *College*, calls this the basic book library and recommends that it include "those original, classic sources and contemporary writings that relate to general and specialized education in the baccalaureate program." This means that the basic collection must reflect the breadth of general education and the depth of each academic department. Everything from the Greek classics to contemporary issues in psychology must be a part of the most rudimentary collection.

Every institution—from the largest to the smallest— must have, at its core, this essential collection of "basic books" that meets the diverse needs of undergraduate students. But how can parents and prospective students tell if the library has satisfied this first criterion of quality? It is not possible, of course, to review every book, but there are other ways to discover if the collection is adequate.

First, look at the library's budget. Specifically, find out how much it spends, per student, on acquisition of new materials and its staff. With these figures, you can compare the commitment of the different colleges and universities you consider. The library staffs of the different institutions should know these figures. Also, ask current students and faculty what they think of the library. Does it have the materials they need? Is a trip to the library a rewarding, or frustrating, experience? How often do they use the library? Their opinions may offer the most important insight of all.

There are other ways to examine the quality of the library's collection. Evan Farber, a nationally recognized expert on academic libraries, says a good library will listen to student opinions and frequently buy books they recommend. Does the library encourage—either formally or informally—student comments about the quality of its collection? Does it buy books because they were suggested by students? These simple questions may reveal a true commitment to undergraduates.

Some college and university libraries also have special programs that monitor the quality of the core collection. At the University of Scranton in Scranton, Pennsylvania, for example, teachers and librarians work as a team to build a collection that meets the specific needs of undergraduates. "We agree together to focus on student needs rather than faculty interest," says librarian Bonnie Strohl. In this era of cutbacks, the University of Scranton is funding a $1.5-million addition to the core collection. Before adding new titles, library staff members compared their collection against holdings of similar libraries and also surveyed students to locate gaps. "We identified areas where they were not able to complete their research because titles were not available or the subject areas were not strong," says Strohl.

Access to Other Libraries

Finally, find out if other libraries are located nearby. A small library may not be a handicap if students have easy access to other academic libraries. Indeed, some small colleges assume their students will use the resources of larger institutions. Among these cooperating libraries, borrowing privileges are shared, allowing full access to the collection and support from library staff.

The City University of New York in New York City, for example, offers the resources of its own well-stocked libraries. But students also have access to the famous New York Public Library. Its 6 million volumes are available for reference use by students and faculty. Also available are the resources of other college and university libraries in the city.

If a college talks about its proximity to another library, find out if, in fact, it is convenient for students to use. Is regular transportation provided? Equally important, ask if students are taught how to locate and use the resources of these cooperating institutions. Although students are often taught how to make good use of their own library, they are typically left to fend for themselves when they travel to another institution.

Is the library's computer technology up to date?

Quality is measured not just by a library's size, but also by its ability to connect students to information far beyond its own walls. Computer databases and the Internet are now considered necessary tools for research.

Books are still essential, but computers have fundamentally altered how students work. Today, they use increasingly sophisticated technology to research and retrieve information stored halfway around the world at the touch of a button. Most breathtaking is the pace of this change. For anyone from an earlier generation, a visit to the modern academic library can be a disorienting experience. The card catalog (now usually computerized) is still important. But there is a bewildering array of new tools and a confusing new vocabulary: Dozens of specialized databases offer direct links by computer to documents on nearly any subject. CD-ROMs allow students to quickly search periodical indexes. The Internet is becoming the most important resource of all, allowing students to send e-mail, track down government data, casually browse the World Wide Web, and much more.

Tools Every College Should Offer

This technology offers more than a new source of information—it is altering the definition of a library. Librarians must now focus not just on acquisition of information—buying books to put on a shelf, for example— but on access to information in many different forms from many different sources. Libraries are still repositories of knowledge, but they are also a kind of information switchboard, providing the technology and expertise needed to connect students to information sitting on a shelf or in a computer terminal far away.

Almost every college or university library is, in some way, now a part of this information network. But how much is enough? There is no one checklist of quality, but all good li-braries should offer students a variety of ways to search for information electronically. There should be access to comput-erized indexes and on-line databases for each of the major dis-ciplines, for example. Also, the best libraries will offer students access to the Internet and the World Wide Web.

Some libraries have made a major investment in this kind of technology. Arizona State University in Tempe, for example, offers students 24-hour access to thirty databases from around the nation. Five of its seven libraries have CD-ROM and other technology that allow students to track down references through the computer. The university also has a 121,000-square-foot "electronic village" that incorporates multimedia classrooms, computer workstations, support staff, and a technical library. University officials assert it is the largest center of its kind. All of this is in addition to the 3 million volumes held by the institution.

Not all libraries are so large, or need to be. Western Connecticut State University in Danbury holds 175,000 volumes in its library. But through a computer link to three other libraries in the state's university system, students have access to approximately 600,000 volumes.

The library should also make good use of interlibrary loans. This service allows students to borrow books or get copies of journal articles held in another library. Ask current students or faculty if it is user-friendly. For example, do students order materials by filling out a simple form, or is the procedure more time-consuming and complicated? How long does it take for ordered materials to arrive? Are students asked to pay for this service? Although some colleges pass along charges to students, others absorb the cost of this service and the student pays nothing.

Connecting Libraries to Residence Halls and Classrooms

Finally, can students go on-line from classrooms and residence halls? At many colleges and universities, students, using their own computers connected to a campuswide network, now search the library's card catalog, send e-mail to their professors, or gain access to the full resources of the Internet from their own rooms or a growing number of "electronic classrooms."

In 1983, Stevens Institute of Technology in Hoboken, New Jersey, was the first college to require students to own personal computers and among the first to install a high-speed network connecting the library to all dormitory rooms. Many colleges and universities followed their lead. Today, students at institutions around the country can complete research and gather a wide range of documents from their own computers. At Whitworth College in Spokane, Washington, every dorm room is being connected to a new fiber-optic network allowing students to go on-line to exchange e-mail and complete research at any hour of the day or night. They call their initiative "a port for every pillow." At California Polytechnic State University in San Luis Obispo, students can connect to the library through their computer on campus or at home. Once on-line, they can search the library catalog, get copies of material held on reserve by faculty, and even communicate with reference librarians when they have a question.

Classrooms are also going on-line. At Pennsylvania State University in University Park, sixty classrooms are now equipped with computer technology. Faculty can project information and pictures, ranging from digital images of Renaissance art to the latest national weather map, reports Terry Morrow, a fellow at the Center for Academic Computing. "It's changing the whole concept of how you teach," he says.

The University of Washington in Seattle is also bringing computers into the classroom. Its "model classroom of the future" allows students to plug their laptop computers into a campuswide network and work collaboratively on group projects. This technology and the service of interlibrary loan means even the smallest and most isolated institution has access to a growing and increasingly important global information network. Students now take for granted their ability to send messages around the world instantaneously or to download a journal article while sitting in bed. In the classroom, slides and overhead projectors are being replaced by computer terminals connected directly to the library—and beyond.

Will Computers Replace Books?

This technology, however, can be overused. Be cautious if an institution brushes aside any concern for the quality of its own library collection by saying, "You can get that through the Internet." This may be true, especially in the sciences and several other disciplines. But there is no substitute for a strong core collection of books and journals. Electronic communication supports the work of libraries, but it is not yet a satisfactory substitute for the information kept on nearby shelves. In fact, the wonders of the Internet are easily overstated. Some experts talk with excitement about "virtual libraries," where all information will be stored electronically, eliminating the need for paper and buildings. But no such institution yet exists.

"More and more information will be available on-line," says library expert Evan Farber. "It's increasing every day. But much material won't be on-line for decades, if ever. Think of all the millions of books that have been published since the 1500s that are not going to be put in electronic form." Students will still use books, he concludes, and a library still needs to maintain a strong collection of print material. For now, electronic communication plays an important, but supporting, role.

Are students taught how to use the library and make good use of the information they collect?

At a college of quality, librarians teach students how to find the information they need, and library instruction is part of the undergraduate curriculum. In addition, professional librarians are available during all open hours to answer questions.

Even a well-stocked library holding all the latest technology will frustrate students if they have not been taught how to locate information. All good libraries will be staffed with librarians who make time to help students. It is impossible to overstate the importance of librarians. A professional, dedicated staff is the one truly indispensable resource in any library. They do far more than shelve books; they are teachers and essential guides, helping students locate the most useful books, track down the latest journal articles, and make the best use of on-line research. Equally important, librarians help students pick the right information and use it wisely.

This teaching role should formally begin during the freshman year. New students should be taught how to locate and use the library's card catalog and indexes and then how to find needed books and articles. Most colleges and universities offer a library orientation during new student week. But many librarians feel this is not enough. Instead, students should have the opportunity to spend even more time in the library, learning to find information and use its electronic resources.

At some colleges, formal for-credit courses are offered in library use. At the State University of New York College at Plattsburg, for example, all students enroll in "Introduction to Library Research." At other institutions, library instruction is incorporated into other classes, such as freshman seminars or English composition courses.

At the University of Nevada at Las Vegas, students enrolled in a required composition course are asked to write a paper using information gathered from library research. To prepare for the assignment, librarians teach students how to use the latest technology, including databases and the World Wide Web, according to Lori Temple, associate vice provost for academic affairs. Students come the library, work on the computers, and see firsthand how to locate the information they need. "The composition instructor and the librarian work together to help the students understand how to find the information they need and produce the kind of reports and papers required for the course," she explains.

Librarians Help Students Find the Right Information

Students learn how to operate the computers, of course, but they are also taught how to be efficient scholars. Computers allow access to a vast amount of information, much of it poorly organized. If students do not know how to ask the right questions or look in the right places, they may end up with too much information that has little value. "You have to learn how to limit [computer] searches, otherwise you spend an enormous amount of time and end up with articles you may not need or use," explains Temple.

Beth L. Mark, a librarian at Messiah College in Grantham, Pennsylvania, also emphasizes this need to be selective. "When I went to school, sometimes it was hard to find enough information. Now we emphasize how to narrow down [computer searches] because 10,000 articles could easily pop up." At Messiah College, library instruction is a formal part of the freshman seminar. Each class is assigned a librarian who works closely with the instructor, says Mark. "We focus all our instruction around the teachers' assignments and their topics." For example, students studying immigration may be asked to compare a current article on the subject with another written before 1950. In this way, classwork and library instruction are seamlessly connected.

Librarians Must Be Accessible

At the best colleges and universities, librarians teach in the classroom. But also make sure the library is adequately staffed with librarians available to answer questions and locate useful books and articles. There must be professional reference librarians on duty during most open hours. In addition, librarians must be accessible—not hidden away from students in distant offices.

When visiting a library, look for a reference librarian. Can one be found in a public place, accessible to students? Are they helping students find the information they need? Or are they working behind a closed door or at a large, intimidating desk, unavailable to all but the most determined students?

Librarians are teachers. They should, therefore, be treated like teachers. When visiting a college or university, it is worthwhile to ask one more question: Are librarians faculty members? The distinction between staff and faculty may appear subtle, but it is important. If librarians are faculty members, it means they are full members of the academic community. They take part in faculty committees and are usually eligible for tenure. All this allows them to grow professionally and contribute their knowledge to the whole institution.

At Aurora University in Aurora, Illinois, for example, librarians are faculty, and according to library director Susan Craig, this gives them a stronger voice on campus. "They are included in everything. They are on committees and are part of the decision-making process with the curriculum," she says. Students may not notice the difference when they walk into the library, but in the end, the whole institution is made stronger when librarians are made equal partners in the campus.

Does the library offer other kinds of resources for learning?

Not all knowledge can be contained in a library. Botancal gardens, art collections, or historical artifacts are, in their own way, also repositories of useful information.

This chapter puts the spotlight on the library. But many colleges and universities offer other kinds of resources for learning. For example, a college-run museum or arboretum is a library of another sort. It does not contain books, but it does hold information used in research.

Cornell University in Ithaca, New York, maintains Cornell Plantations, a "museum of living plants" adjacent to the campus. According to Joel Seligman, director of campus information, the 2,900-acre arboretum, botanical garden, and nature preserve is a living laboratory used in many undergraduate courses. "Students go to the plantation as part of their regular classes," he says. They may investigate plant life as part of a biology lab, for example, and identify different ecological systems. The university recently completed a path through the plantation that features markers along the route describing plant life and its geological history. Even a casual stroll through campus can give students a better understanding of the natural world.

Baker University in Baldwin City, Kansas, maintains 600 acres of wetlands, woods, and prairie near its campus. According to John Fuller, director of news services, the site "allows for hands-on study of everything from native plants to endangered species." The university recently added degrees in environmental chemistry, environmental technology and management, and wildlife biology. For these students, the university land is an especially useful resource.

The University of Findlay in Findlay, Ohio, holds as part of its collection original works of art from children's books. Students from elementary schools regularly visit the collection, university officials report, but it is also a resource for students pursuing degrees in elementary education and art.

Other colleges maintain observatories, historical museums, artifacts from different cultures, and much more. All of this can enrich course work and research. Find out if these resources are accessible to undergraduate students. For example, is an arboretum used as a resource in undergraduate courses? Have historical artifacts been studied by students for research projects? Like a library, students must be introduced to these collections and shown how to make

133

good use of the information they contain. The library is an essential part of undergraduate education. It is a resource all students must use if they are to get the most from their college experience. It should be inviting and support a collection that meets the needs of students.

A library should also make students "information literate." When students know how to independently find and use information, they are prepared for a lifetime of learning. The American Library Association puts it this way: "Ultimately, information-literate people are those who have learned how to learn. They know how to learn because they know how knowledge is organized, how to find information, and how to use information." (Presidential Committee on Information Literacy, Final Report, 1989). Society is changing so rapidly that much of what we learn today will soon be out of date. To keep pace with this change—as both workers and citizens—everyone must continue his or her education. In this way, the ability to find information is no less important than the information itself.

During the early twentieth century, the wealthy industrialist Andrew Carnegie financed the construction of nearly 1,700 public libraries throughout the Americas. For him they were "universities of the people," and he believed they had the power to elevate society. Today, the value of knowledge has only grown. We now talk about a new division in the nation separating the "information rich" from the "information poor." Those with information have influence and power. Those without grow more powerless.

In America, higher education is expected to break down barriers to opportunity. To succeed in this mission, all colleges and universities must help students prepare for a lifetime of learning—help them "learn how to learn." Therefore, the library—too often put on the fringes of academic life—might be the most essential aspect of higher education.

The Key Questions to Ask

The library should be an essential part of every college and university campus. It should have a a helpful, professional staff and a collection that meets the research needs of undergraduate students.

1. Does the library serve the needs of undergraduate students?

- What does the library spend annually on acquisitions and staff pcr student? How does this compare with other institutions you are considering?
- Are students and staff happy with the library? Can they identify gaps in the collection?
- Does the library buy books recommended by students? Does it encourage student opinion in other ways?
- Do students have easy access to other college or university libraries?

2. How advanced is the library's computer technology?

- Does the library offer computerized indexes and on-line databases for each of the major academic disciplines?
- Is the library connected to the Internet and World Wide Web?
- Are classrooms and dormitories also connected to a campuswide computer nctwork?
- Does the library offer interlibrary loan? Is this service easy to use and free?

3. Are students taught how to use library resources?

- Is library instruction a formal part of the undergraduate curriculum?

- Is the library staffed with reference librarians during all open hours?
- Are librarians considered faculty members?

4. **Does the college or university offer other resources for learning?**
   - Are botanical gardens, art museums, historical collections, or other artifacts part of the institution's collection?
   - Are these resources used in undergraduate instruction?

7

Extending the Campus

Our romantic image of the typical college student—a person between the ages of 18 and 21, who lives on campus and studies full-time—now represents only 20 percent of the total college population. Today, the "typical" student is often older and takes, on average, six years to finish an undergraduate degree.

Many colleges and universities are adapting to these changing demographics. They allow students to study part-time, in the evenings, on weekends, and even from a distance. It is now possible, for example, to earn a degree without ever stepping on a college campus—students study independently and complete classes through video, correspondence, and computer instruction. These opportunities make college accessible to more people than ever before. It is now possible to fit higher education into even the busiest schedule.

More institutions now allow students to design their own majors and pursue independent study projects. A growing number of schools offer credit for "life experience"—knowledge and skills gained through work, travel, and self-study. In this way, colleges are willing to personalize the curriculum to suit the interests of individual students.

Not every student needs—or wants—this kind of flexibility. But a college that works to meet the changing needs of students and acknowledges their unique interests is making an important statement. In ways both large and small, this effort reflects a belief that students come before the institution. In other words, education should be organized for the benefit of students, not just the convenience of the college.

Giving Students a Voice

Today, these are typical college students:

- A middle-aged women in Maryland returns to school, hoping to earn a business degree and find a new career. "I want to get ahead in the business environment, not stay stagnant," she explains. A special weekend-only program allows her to keep her job and still get a degree. After nearly six years of study, she is about to graduate.
- Several states away, another student is completing a major created just for him. He enrolled in college to study engineering, but his interest turned to the specialized field of sports medicine. Instead of turning him away, the university helped design a custom-made major through internships and independent study projects.
- Meanwhile, a university student in Texas recently completed independent research in the jungles of Costa Rica. Working on his own, he learned essential scientific skills and a self-confidence no professor could teach. "In the jungle, there is no professor looking over your shoulder telling you what to do or how to do it," he explains. The results of his work have already been published in a book.

These and millions of other students are learning in ways that were rare only a generation ago and not even imagined when Harvard and other colonial colleges brought higher education to America in the seventeenth century. Each example reflects a growing emphasis on flexibility in the undergraduate curriculum. Students have more opportunity to set the terms of their education. Many earn credit through independent study and design their own majors. Part-time, weekend, and evening programs let students mix school with work and family. Computer and video technology allow them to learn from almost any location.

When Students Become Customers

The trends just described reflect dramatic changes in the student population. Many are older; most work—often full-time—and expect college to satisfy their unique needs and interests. "For the majority of students," reported the Institute for Research on Higher Education at the University of Pennsylvania, "college is not a 'rite of passage,' not a traditional sprint through four years of hurdles from high school to the college diploma" (*Change*, September/October 1993). Instead, college is now seen by students of all ages as a branch of the service industry, to use as needed throughout a lifetime. As customers, students expect colleges to give them exactly what they want, when they want it.

Some educators worry about this trend. If learning is seen as little more than a product to buy, then the full richness of college may be lost and the whole notion of higher education cheapened. On the other hand, this movement reflects the best qualities of a democratic nation. It is a uniquely American belief that higher education should serve the practical needs of the people and be accessible to all. A willingness—even eagerness—to serve students of all ages and interests is actually part of a more than century long effort to make college available and meaningful to an ever-larger number of citizens.

In this chapter, we help you identify colleges and universities that allow flexibility in the educational process. The programs are diverse. Some focus on adult learners; others accommodate the creativity and enthusiasm of traditional students. But all prove that a quality education can also adapt to different students and respond to individual needs. When this flexibility is matched with high academic expectations and careful supervision, a new and exciting vision for higher learning emerges.

Do students design their own majors?

Most colleges and universities allow students to earn credit through independent study. But some make a special commitment to individualized learning. They offer interdisciplinary majors and allow students to design their own majors from scratch.

The largest universities may offer more than 100 different majors. But at some colleges and universities, the list of possible majors is limited only by each student's imagination. At Denison University in Granville, Ohio, for example, students have majored in subjects ranging from "Third-World Geography" to "Imagination and Human Behavior." These programs are not listed in the university's catalog; instead, each was created by students through the Individually Designed Major Program.

Associate provost Keith Boone cautions that this program is more rigorous than standard majors. More than a collection of interesting classes, a self-designed major must have the same depth and coherence of any other major. Each must be carefully designed and then approved by a faculty committee. "Students have to really jump through the hoops," he says.

If it's harder, why do students bother? "Students who choose this option are independent thinkers, they're bright, and they are the kind of students who don't see themselves locked into a standard major," Boone says. "They have enough intellectual independence that they would like to construct their own program." Typically, these students also know exactly what they want to study and hope to turn their interest into a career. "This is their interest and always has been, and they want to major in it," says Boone. "But they are also looking forward to going into a specific profession. They feel like this will serve them well."

Alfred University in Alfred, New York, offers a similar opportunity for students who want to blaze their own trails.

Through its program, called Track II, students have studied subjects ranging from American diplomacy to biomedical photography. "Anything with substantial academic and intellectual content is fair game," says David Meisner, a member of the psychology department faculty who advises Track II students.

"I don't want to make it sound like anything can be done," he says, "but we try to emphasize alternative ways of learning." Students are encouraged to earn credit through independent study, work with a faculty mentor, study abroad, internships, or by taking a course at another institution. Because students can use resources and expertise found off campus, their choice of majors is almost unlimited. Students in Track II work with an adviser and also with a handpicked faculty committee. These faculty members help students create their majors and also monitor their progress. "The program works best for students who are really good at taking initiative," says Meisner, but the advisory board helps the student shape the program of study and determine where and how the student will study.

Clearly, the self-designed major is not for everyone. At Denison University, only about 4 percent of students choose to chart their own course. At Alfred, only a few students complete a Track II program each year. But for those who do, students are given the necessary support and guidance needed to make it a successful experience.

Students who design their own majors often discover other benefits. By taking charge of their learning, they also think about what it means to be educated: What is essential knowledge? How does their subject relate to other disciplines? What are the best ways to learn? "Students really think through the whole process as they're putting their program together," confirms Director of Admissions Laurie Richer.

Self-designed Majors No Longer a Rarity

When investigating a college or university, ask if students are allowed to create their own majors. Also ask: What percentage of students take advantage of this opportunity? How is a program developed and approved? A student should be allowed to develop a unique program of study, but he or she should also be carefully guided during the process.

These kinds of programs were once rare and considered experimental. But today, many institutions allow students to shape their own course of study. Indeed, a few colleges expect every student to create an individualized major. Goddard College in Plainfield, Vermont, was an early leader in nontraditional learning. There, all students piece together their own unique program by selecting courses from five broad subject areas.

At other institutions, self-designed majors are an option. At the University of Missouri–Columbia, an interdisciplinary studies degree is offered through the Office of Special Degree Programs. Kent State University in Ohio allows students enrolled in its Honors College to create self-designed programs. Vassar College in Poughkeespie, New York, offers four routes to a bachelor's degree, including an interdepartmental program, a multidisciplinary program, and an independently designed major.

Is credit awarded for independent study?

Are students encouraged to earn credit through independent study? Do students prepare for life after college through internships or cooperative education programs?

Typically completed in the junior or senior year, independent study projects allow students to investigate, on their own, a subject relevant to their major. Bloomsburg University in Bloomsburg, Pennsylvania, is just one of many institutions that allow, and often require, students to complete independent study projects. In the past, students there have earned credit for photography projects, biological research, the study of literature, and more.

Colleges usually limit the amount of independent study credit a student may earn. At most institutions, independent study supplements—not replaces—the regular curriculum. But independent study is still an important part of learning. It allows students to fill gaps in the curriculum, pursue subjects of personal interest, and take charge of their education. Not every student will pursue learning through independent study. But a college or university that offers this kind of learning gives students more options. Make sure independent study is allowed and find out how actively it is supported. What percentage of undergraduate students earn credit in this way?

Internships: Putting Theory into Practice

Students on many campuses also earn credit through internships. At some institutions, an internship may be required for graduation. Usually completed off campus, often during summer months, internships allow students to practice what they have learned in the classroom and, in many cases, get valuable job-related experience.

At Converse College in Spartansburg, South Carolina, for example, internships are expected to help students prepare for a career. "The internship blends the theoretical knowledge of the classroom with the practical knowledge of the world of work," says JoAnne Lever, dean of the college of arts and sciences. "We think internships are extremely valuable, both for career decision making and for providing

career-related work experience," she explains. "It's important for students to know what they want to do, but it's also
important for them to know what they don't want to do.
Internships help them with both of those."

At this college, all internships are coordinated by an
office of career services. It provides a list of available
internships and works to make a good match. In the past,
students have worked for newspapers, accountants, lawyers,
legislators, and corporations. Overall, about half of Converse
College students graduate with some internship experience.

At Colby College in Waterville, Maine, a network of
alumni, parents, and friends help students find internships
that suit their unique interests. There is also a discretionary
fund that pays for special projects. Recently funded projects
include a trip to Mississippi to research dialects for a play and
study in Bosnia. "The sky and a student's imagination are the
limits," the college reports.

Ideally, students should have the flexibility to find an
internship that suits their special interests. But they should
also be guided and supported by faculty or college staff.
When evaluating a college or university's commitment to
student internships, find out how many students take part in
one or more internships. Also ask how students are guided
when selecting an internship and how the experience is
evaluated. Are they expected to write a paper or share what
they have learned in other ways?

Cooperative Education: Making the Workplace a Classroom

Finally, many colleges offer a program that more fully blends
classroom study and work experience. Cooperative education—or "co-op ed"—is a popular program that places
students in a job where they earn both a paycheck and

academic credit. This program allows students to gain practical on-the-job experience and helps pay for the cost of their education.

At some colleges and universities, students work part-time for a year or less. At other institutions, co-op education defines their college experience; they may be employed full-time for as many as three years.

Formed in 1912, the cooperative education program at the Rochester Institute of Technology in Rochester, New York, is one of the nation's oldest and largest. There, more than 1,300 co-op employers serve over 2,600 students a year. Students find work in local businesses, Fortune 500 companies, government, and nonprofit corporations around the country and in thirty other nations. Hundreds of other colleges and universities offer their own cooperative education programs. Weber State University in Ogden, Utah, serves approximately 4,800 students each year who extend their classroom into 3,000 businesses nationwide. At the Laboratory of Merchandising in New York City, students work full-time during three of their four years. Their experiences are documented in papers and oral presentations and are discussed in monthly seminars.

Where and when do students take classes?

Can students study part-time? Are evening and weekend courses offered for those needing more flexibility? Is credit awarded for life experience? If the is answer yes, then the college or university is working hard to accommodate the changing needs of today's students.

College does not have to be a full-time occupation. Today, more than 40 percent of all college students study part-time. Some estimate that this figure will climb to nearly 50 percent by the turn of the century.

Increasingly, colleges and universities offer special programs that cater to the needs of part-time students. For example, many colleges and universities now offer classes in the evening and weekends. Some allow students to complete entire degree programs by attending class during these "off hours."

Weekend Colleges for Nontraditional Students

The College of Notre Dame of Maryland in Baltimore, for example, enrolls about 1,500 students each term in its Weekend College. According to director Sister Pamela Jablon, the program serves students who cannot—or prefer not to—study during the workweek. Students of all ages are welcome, but it is especially attractive to working adults. Why do they go back to college? "For the majority, it is personal satisfaction," says Sister Jablon. "But there are other motivations. They want to advance in their jobs—maybe they're trying to keep their jobs—or change careers."

Standing in the lobby of the Weekend College's own administration and classroom building, Sister Jablon describes what a college education means to many of its students. "It's an oasis to come here," she says. "They have such hectic lives. They view coming here as peace and quiet"—an opportunity to do something for themselves. Around her, students walk between classes and chat in small groups, looking very much like college students anywhere. Like most weekend college programs, career-oriented majors are most popular. Students can study business, elementary education, human services, and computer information systems. But majors in liberal arts and religious studies are also offered, reflecting the diverse interests of students.

Established more than twenty years ago, this Weekend College is nationally recognized. However, there are similar programs around the country. Lourdes College in Sylvania, Ohio, has its own Weekend College. At Spalding University in Louisville, Kentucky, about 190 students earn a degree through four or five years of weekend-only study.

Earning Credit for Life Experience

At these and similar institutions, students attend class at nontraditional times. But, just as important, they also learn in nontraditional ways. Part-time and weekend programs are more likely to accept credits earned at other colleges and universities. They may also allow students to earn additional credits by passing equivalency exams, such as CLEP (College-Level Examination Program). Some also award academic credit for "life experience"—skills and knowledge gained through work or self-study.

Many traditional colleges and universities reject the academic value of life experience. However, a growing number of educators understand that students are not blank slates. Many arrive on campus with a set of skills and experiences that equal—or exceed—what is taught in the classroom. When this knowledge can be demonstrated through careful documentation and thoughtful self-evaluation, credit is given.

At the College of Notre Dame of Maryland, students can prepare a portfolio describing skills learned on their own. "Most is on-the-job training," explains Sister Jablon. "It could be in computers or writing for business. Some students have taught as volunteers. They may have extensive experience." If these skills are deemed college level, then academic credit is awarded.

At Spalding University, one student recently earned credit for his work as a playwright. "He's very good," says Weekend College director David Barnes. "He's had plays produced around the country, but he didn't have any college degree. As part of a portfolio, he submitted some of the plays he's written, which is exactly what you would do in a class." Another student earned credit for his work as a DJ at a local radio station.

Credit for life experience is not limited to weekend or part-time programs. Montana State University–Northern in Havre, Montana, awards credit through its Learning Experience Assessment Program. Participants develop a portfolio documenting learning from life experiences. A full 25 percent of degree requirements may be met in this way, reports registrar Robert McCluskey.

Almost every college requires students to earn a minimum number of credits at their own institution. But when colleges accept credit earned from other institutions, examinations, and life experience, many students are—quite literally—halfway to their degrees. Even when students study part-time or on weekends, they are often able to finish a bachelor's degree in three or four years.

If these programs look attractive, search for an institution best able to satisfy your schedule and academic interests. Larger universities and "commuter colleges" are more likely to offer flexible programs. These institutions are usually located in or near urban areas, have many nonresidential students and, as a general rule, offer more vocational and professional degrees. However, many smaller residential colleges are now adding special programs for part-time and adult students. If you have taken classes at another institution, find out how much credit the college or university you are considering will accept. Too many institutions place unnecessary restrictions on the amount or kind of credit they will accept from other colleges and universities. Likewise, ask if the institution will grant credit for life experience or learning demonstrated though proficiency examinations.

Three-Year Degrees for Students in a Hurry

These programs meet the special needs of adult students. But many traditional college students are also attracted by flexible schedules. Frequently, a traditional student will take more than four years to complete a degree. There are, however, a few institutions that will help students who are in a hurry to graduate. For the ambitious student, it is possible to earn a bachelor's degree in three years.

The three-year degree does not require fewer courses; rather, the same amount of work is squeezed into a shorter time period. Students study more intensively during the academic year and, usually, must also continue earning credit during the summer. Middlebury College in Middlebury, Vermont, for example, now offers a three-year degree in international studies. This program, which focuses on language study and travel abroad, lets students graduate in two summers and three academic years.

This intensive program is not for everyone. Students begin their work in the summer, immediately after they graduate from high school, and they carry an especially heavy academic load. But, according to college officials, students are rewarded for their dedication. "Students who complete this major will be exceptionally well-prepared for a career," reports Clara Chu, vice president for languages. No less enticing, students—and their parents—will save nearly $20,000 over the cost of a traditional four-year degree from that institution.

Is distance learning an option?

The venerable "correspondence course" has grown and matured, thanks to video and computer technology. Today, students can study and communicate with faculty from nearly anywhere in the world.

Most instruction still takes place in a classroom. But a growing number of students take classes and earn entire degrees without stepping on a college or university campus. By one estimate, 4 million Americans are now taking classes through distance learning. These students study independently at their own pace, and they stay in touch with professors by mail, phone, or computer.

Correspondence study has existed for more than a century, but video and computer technology is responsible for the movement's explosive growth. It is now possible to study everything from creative writing to business administration by sitting at a home computer or watching videotaped lectures. Students attend "classes," send assignments, and talk with instructors electronically. Some colleges and universities broadcast classes via satellite to remote classrooms around a state or region. Students watch an instructor on interactive television and, typically, have an opportunity to ask questions even when they are hundreds of miles away.

Other distance learners earn credit by reading assigned books, viewing videotapes, writing papers, taking proctored tests, and completing independent projects. They may communicate with professors and, increasingly, other students, by phone or e-mail. The University of Wisconsin and the University of Southern Utah, for example, offer many courses in this manner. Students take classes for personal enjoyment or as part of a degree program. A growing number of colleges and universities allow students to earn most or all credit needed for a degree through independent study. At the University of Wisconsin–Green Bay, for example, its Extended Degree Program now enrolls about 400 students who complete most of their requirements off campus. Face-to-face meetings with faculty are scheduled once or twice during a semester, but students complete most course work on their own.

Colleges without Campuses

There are also a number of well-regarded "colleges without walls" devoted entirely to distance learning. These institutions do not have a traditional campus and offer no classes of their own. Instead, students earn credit for life experience, independent study, internships, and course work completed at other institutions.

At Empire State College, part of the State University of New York system, students work individually with faculty mentors to plan a degree program that suits their needs. Other colleges without walls include Thomas Edison State College in Trenton, New Jersey, and Regents College, also located in New York.

Distance learning is an alternative approach to learning, but the most successful courses and degrees still duplicate what the best traditional colleges offer: personal support from faculty and staff, a thoughtful and creative curriculum, and—to the greatest extent possible—a sense of community and mutual support from other students. If you are interested in nontraditional courses or degree programs, make sure the schools you are considering try to satisfy all of the ten criteria described in this book. The methods will, of course, be different, but the commitment to students should be just as strong.

Colleges without walls were created specifically for nontraditional students. But the philosophy of learning that these alternative colleges pioneered twenty or thirty years ago is now being adopted in many traditional colleges and universities. As the number of students climb and the cost of higher education grows, more and more institutions will take advantage of new technology to serve even the most traditional college student.

At the University of Missouri–St. Louis, for example, students may use interactive video when taking courses on subjects ranging from nursing to Korean language. Writing assignments may be sent to professors at any hour of the day or night via computer. "What we are trying to do is use technology as another tool," explains university communications director Bob Samples. And it is changing how everyone learns. He predicts that more and more students, of all ages and backgrounds, will learn through independent study, by computer, even from the home.

All of this activity answers America's insatiable appetite for education. "Learning is addictive; the more education people have, the more they seem to want," K. Patricia Cross, an expert in adult education, accurately predicted in a 1980 issue of *Phi Delta Kappan*. As colleges and universities work to satisfy this demand, they are creating new ways of learning that benefit all students.

The Key Questions to Ask

Higher education is finding new ways to serve students. From internships to nontraditional degree programs, colleges have become more flexible and inclusive.

1. **Do students design their own majors?**
   - What percentage of students design their own programs of study?
   - How is the program supervised by faculty?

2. **Is credit awarded for independent study?**
   - Are students allowed—perhaps even encouraged—to earn credit through independent study projects?
   - Are internships also allowed?

- Does the college help students find appropriate internships, and does it supervise their progress?
- Is a cooperative education program offered for students who want to combine college study with experience in the workforce?

3. **Where and when do students take classes?**
    - Do students study part-time?
    - Are evening and/or weekend programs available for those needing more flexibility?
    - Is credit awarded for life experience? Is credit earned at other institutions honored?
    - Is it possible to earn a degree in less than four years?

4. **Is distance learning an option?**
    - Is it possible to take courses through correspondence study?
    - How are these courses or degrees taught?
    - Do students have easy access to professors and college services, even when they learn off campus?

8

College Life

One of the oldest and most persistent traditions in American higher education is that college is expected to become each student's second home. The first colleges in America accepted their roles as surrogate parents, often with excessive zeal. In that Puritan era, every aspect of a young student's life was regulated and monitored. From morning chapel to the evening meal, young scholars were expected to follow elaborate codes of conduct. Professors would spy through windows and listen at keyholes, looking for infractions.

This kind of moral policework was abandoned long ago at most institutions. Students today will probably not encounter anyone like the nineteenth-century college president who watched students during chapel by praying with one eye open or the distinguished economics professor who chased a student running off with a stolen turkey.

But all colleges and universities still accept responsibility for the safety of their students and work to create a caring, supportive community. In *loco parentis* has been all but abandoned, but educators still want their campuses to be places where students can grow socially and intellectually.

A good college or university, then, will offer more than a strong academic program. It will encourage students to work together and become leaders on campus. Guest speakers, all-college forums, dance presentations, and more will be part of campus life.

Building Community

How do college students spend their free time? "Don't tell me," many parents are tempted to respond. "I don't want to know."

There is, certainly, no shortage of horror stories. News reports regularly describe the underbelly of college life: Drug and alcohol use, sexual mischief, and crime of all sorts. College, once seen as a safe haven, is now treated more like a minefield, filled with hidden dangers. In response, consumers—and even government officials—are asking hard questions about the quality and safety of campus life. Federal legislation now requires most colleges and universities to report their crime rates and create security policies. Parents want to know how, precisely, their children's safety is guarded. "It isn't the way it was five years ago when parents just wanted to be reassured," said one campus director of public safety in a *New York Times* article (January 7, 1996).

The emphasis on safety is good news, but a healthy campus is defined by more than the absence of crime. The best institutions also build a sense of community. For students, time spent out of class is just as meaningful as the time spent in class, and all members are treated with respect. At these institutions, students may use their free time to attend a lecture by a Nobel laureate, participate in a student-produced play, chat with faculty in a residence hall lounge, participate in intramural sports, or write for the school newspaper. Leadership skills will be nurtured within student government and in student organizations across campus. There are also special programs for commuter students and other nontraditional learners.

Of course, not every hour must be filled with prepackaged, wholesome activities. But students should be offered a wide range of opportunities in order to grow socially and intellectually. Research confirms that students who feel connected to their college or university by getting involved in extracurricular work and building friendships are more likely to succeed academically and earn a degree.

In this chapter, we help you identify colleges and universities that build this vital sense of community, creating an environment for learning where all students are not only safe, but also treated with respect and are intellectually challenged inside and outside of the classroom.

Is the campus safe?

Every college and university must build a community where all of its members are treated with respect and live without undo fear. Campus security must be a priority, and every student should abide by a clearly stated code of conduct.

Americans worry about crime, but until recently, college and university campuses were seen as islands of tranquility. It was enough to know that campus police were on the beat, and residence halls were locked at night. This is no longer the case. Highly publicized student murders and growing attention to other types of crime—especially rape—has reminded the nation that personal safety is never guaranteed. Colleges and universities, like all communities, must protect its members.

Many are working harder to guard personal safety. Escort services, for example, are now common on many campuses; campus police or volunteers are available to accompany students who must walk across campus at night. Many schools have increased security in residence halls and other buildings. Others educate students about crime by distributing brochures and booklets.

The Incidence of Crime

In addition, most colleges and universities are now required by law to report the incidence of crime on their campuses. After the law was enacted in 1990, Americans had, for the first time, an opportunity to judge the safety of individual campuses. What did the new law reveal? Data from 2,400 colleges were compiled by the *Chronicle of Higher Education* in 1993. As a group, these institutions reported 7,500 incidents of violence when the law took effect in 1992, including 30 murders, nearly 1,000 rapes, and more than 1,800 robberies. Most crimes were less personal; there were more than 32,000 acts of stolen property and nearly 9,000 incidents of motor vehicle theft.

College officials and many education experts, however, caution that this information is not always helpful to consumers. Loopholes in the law allow colleges to ignore some types of crime—such as crimes committed against students living off campus. It makes no distinction between large and small institutions. Also, campuses with the most aggressive security forces often report more crime, not less, because they are better prepared to respond and to keep records.

It is, therefore, unwise and unfair to judge a college by these numbers alone. However, even those who see the law's weaknesses agree that it has helped focus attention on campus crime and has encouraged institutions to seriously look at problems. Every college should comply with the law and make its statistics available to prospective students.

As a next step, find out how the college promotes safety and deters crime. Is there a strong campus security force? Do security officials or other college staff educate students about safety issues? Is the campus well lit at night? If you visit a campus, take the opportunity to ask students there how safe they feel and how well the institution responds to victims of crime.

Codes of Conduct

Campus police are not the only ones responsible for student safety. Students must also be responsible for their own behavior and that of other students. A college becomes a healthy community only when all of its members treat each other with respect. Many colleges have codes of conduct that guide academic conduct. But some colleges make honor codes a meaningful part of college life. At these institutions, students understand the standards for behavior and abide by these rules. Infractions are treated with fairness and consistency.

At Harvey Mudd College, part of the Claremont Colleges in southern California, the honor code was established by students and is run by students. "It applies to all academic matters and to the safety of private and college property," says Gil Villanueva, assistant dean of admissions, meaning that students won't lie, cheat, or steal. Infractions are heard by student-run judiciary and disciplinary boards.

Adherence to the honor code creates more than a safe community; it also allows students to learn in more flexible ways and take full advantage of campus resources at any hour of the day. They have 24-hour access to academic buildings, research labs, and computer equipment without supervision. Professors give take-home exams that are timed and closed book. They also allow students to collaborate on assignments. "For our students, it spells freedom," says Villanueva.

Other colleges have built an atmosphere of trust in similar ways. Rhodes College in Memphis, Tennessee, has a student-governed honor system that administrators and students say is respected. How do they know? "I've seen people fail a take-home test," explained one student in a *Washington Post* article. "That says to me they're not cheating."

When looking at colleges, make sure a clear code of student conduct exists and look for evidence that it is taken seriously by staff, faculty, and students. Do faculty members feel comfortable giving take-home tests or leaving the room when exams are given? Is plagiarism understood? Are personal possessions reasonably safe from opportunistic thieves? How are infractions dealt with? What role do students play in this process?

Campus safety requires more than lights and locks. In the end, it depends on an atmosphere of respect, concern for others, and trust. "Campuses sometimes make a mistake by responding to just one issue, like sexual abuse," says Jim Carr, executive vice-president at Harding University in Searcy, Arkansas. "But if students are taught respect for others, it would solve so many other problems."

Are cultural opportunities offered?

A good college or university offers a variety of concerts, lectures, convocations, and other events that enrich the campus intellectually and culturally.

The Blenders have nothing to do with home economics, and Life in General isn't an interdisciplinary course. They happen to be bands recently touring the college circuit and just two of the approximately sixty events scheduled each year at Winthrop University in Rock Hill, South Carolina. In recent years, the university also booked blues, reggae, gospel, jazz, and classical groups, along with an eclectic variety of novelty acts, including jugglers and hypnotists. Lectures have been presented on everything from racism to the roots of rock and roll. "We have something every Friday and Saturday," says Boyd Jones, who helps organize the entertainment through the university's student union.

What does this have to do with higher education? Jones explains: "Eighty-six percent of our students come from South Carolina. Now there's nothing wrong with being from South Carolina, but maybe they've never heard an Irish folk singer; maybe they've never seen a coffee house act. It's part of developing the whole person, not just Monday to Friday academics."

Colleges As Centers of Culture

Most colleges agree with Boyd Jones. On campuses across the country, students gather to hear a rock band, discuss new research at a departmental tea, listen to a poetry reading, attend a political debate. These institutions become centers of culture, bringing new images, sounds, and ideas in and out of the classroom.

The University of California, Berkeley, for example, supports a diverse community of intellectuals and artists that enrich the campus and the surrounding community. "Learning never stops at Berkeley," assert university officials. "It flourishes not only in the seminar room, laboratory, or library, but also in meeting rooms, residence halls, and coffee houses."

Large universities, like large cities, typically offer more activities. But many small colleges welcome some of the nation's most important scholars, politicians, artists, and performers to their campuses. Little William Jewell College in Liberty, Missouri, notes that its Fine Arts Program has a distinguished history. Luciano Pavarotti made his American recital debut at the college in 1973. Itzhak Perlman, Beverly Sills, the Royal Shakespeare Company, and more have appeared on its stage. In this way, small colleges do not have to be more isolated or more parochial; rather, they can become centers of culture for an entire region.

Other colleges and universities—large and small—take advantage of their urban location. Hunter College, located in the heart of Manhattan, stresses its proximity to such cultural landmarks as Broadway, Lincoln Center, and top art museums. Its New York location gives students easy access to professional artists and musicians, who exhibit work and perform on campus. Likewise, the Newschool of Architecture is located in San Diego's newly designated art district, home to coffee shops and artist studios, where students can gain ideas and inspiration.

Do the colleges and universities that you're considering offer an equally diverse array of cultural activities? Do recent speakers represent a range of views? Do invited artists and performers reflect the rich cultural traditions of America and other nations? Also, do students showcase their own talents by, for example, describing their own research or presenting recitals? If you visit a campus, find out what is being presented that week. How many events would you like to attend?

Are residence halls a place in which to live and learn?

Residence halls—or "dorms"—should help build a sense of community on campus. The best residential colleges and universities support a wide range of social and academic activities. Trained resident advisers and professional staff are available to all students.

Students attending a residential college spend more time in their own room than anywhere else. Yet residence halls are often the most neglected buildings on campus. All but ignored by faculty and administrators, they become isolated enclaves disconnected from the rest of college life. At some colleges and universities, however, residence halls are centers for living and learning. At these institutions, faculty and administrators may hold seminars in halls, and special social and cultural programs will promote a sense of community. Far more than housing, the residence hall is an integral part of the campus.

Living and Learning

Harvard University, for example, offers a unique House System that builds an especially strong sense of community. Freshmen live in dormitories, but most other undergraduates live in one of twelve "houses." Each house is home to approximately 400 students, as well as twenty graduate student tutors and a tenured faculty member, according to Jen Wood from Harvard's Housing Office. There, students eat in a common dining hall, meet with their advisers, attend discussion groups, and organize an impressive range of social activities, from a *Messiah* sing-along to intramural sports. Most students stay in the same house for all three years, creating a stable, cohesive community of learners.

Many colleges and universities are working especially hard to make faculty members more active participants in residential life. Like Harvard, they now encourage faculty to spend time in residence halls and take part in social activities. At Whittier College in Whittier, California, each residence hall is assigned to a Faculty Master, a distinguished senior professor who lives on campus. These faculty members organize a wide range of cultural, social, and educational events for their students. Students have had dinner and conversation with ambassadors, lawyers, doctors, politicians, writers, musicians, and athletes.

Faculty members are also frequent visitors in the residence halls at Baldwin-Wallace College in Berea, Ohio. This college schedules faculty "drop-in hours" in each hall, giving students and teachers an opportunity to meet and visit. No formal presentations are planned; rather, these casual get-togethers are designed to break down the walls separating faculty from student life.

When evaluating a college or university, look for evidence that residence halls are an active part of campus life. How many social and cultural events are held in halls? Do formal programs bring faculty and students together? Community can be strengthened in other ways. Many campuses offer living/learning floors in residence halls, where students who share similar interests live together. At the University of Maryland at College Park, honors students may select from seven themes, including international studies, the arts, and science and environmental studies. At other institutions, living/learning programs are available to all students, usually during the freshman year.

Balancing Independence with Order

Founders of America's early colleges believed dormitories were an essential part of higher education. They assumed the experience would teach young students responsibility and provide scholarly inspiration. Dormitories would be a place where, in the words of education historian Frederick Rudolph, "young men talked deep into the night deeply about deep matters." Unfortunately, the reality was far different. "The dormitory helped to create an atmosphere that invited frustration, argument, and crime," Rudolph writes in *The American College and University: A History*.

He cites an example of dormitory life in the nineteenth century: "In the commons room of a dormitory at South Carolina College in 1833 two students at the same moment grabbed for a plate of trout: one of them survived the duel that ensued."

Today's residence halls are very different places. Most house both sexes. And while many students grumble about roommates, noise, or the building's heating and cooling system, they generally enjoy hall life. For young students leaving home for the first time, it's an opportunity to experience near complete independence and learn social skills.

Most colleges and universities impose some rules for student conduct such as specifying quiet hours, prohibiting alcohol, or limiting visits from nonhall residents. Most schools also place student counselors in each hall to help guide and, when necessary, supervise activity. However, enforcement of these rules and the amount of support and guidance offered varies greatly. At some institutions, the presence of alcohol is cause for expulsion. At others, underage drinking is all but ignored.

If you are considering a residential college, ask about residence hall rules. Is quiet time set aside in the evening and night? What is the policy toward alcohol use? How are these rules enforced? How, specifically, are student counselors trained for the responsibilities they are given? How are they guided and supported by professional staff?

Let's not be naive: Even when college officials say, with conviction, that hall rules are strictly enforced, they are, in fact, usually circumvented and often flagrantly ignored. Stereos blare at all hours and drinking goes on behind closed doors. Don't expect a monastery. But every institution should create an environment where all students are treated with concern and guidance is available when needed.

Does the college or university respect and celebrate diversity on its campus?

A good college or university will attract a student body that reflects the rich diversity of America. Also, international students will be encouraged to contribute fully to the campus culture.

America's colleges and universities have a special responsibility to serve those who have, until recently, been largely left out of higher education. African Americans have struggled for the right to take advantage of higher learning. They, along with Hispanics, Native Americans, and other ethnic minorities, are still underrepresented and often face subtle, but significant, barriers.

The best institutions recruit and retain these students by offering programs that encourage their success. Many schools have an office of minority affairs or discuss racial issues across the campus. But even more important, these colleges must also listen and learn from their students and—in the tradition of American higher education—encourage them to make their mark on the institution. When new students are invited into American higher education, both the students and the institution should grow and change.

Minority students are not the only ones who benefit. Learning is made richer for all when diversity is a priority, argues Harvard University president Neil Rudenstine. "Students benefit in countless ways from the opportunity to live and learn among peers whose perspectives and experiences differ from their own," he writes. It "challenges them to explore ideas and arguments at a deeper level" (*Chronicle of Higher Education*, April 19, 1996). In this way, diversity means more than equal opportunity; it is an essential part of a good education.

Reflection of a Changing Nation

This vision of rich diversity is embraced at Bloomfield College in Bloomfield, New Jersey. At this institution, located near Newark and just south of New York City, 46 percent of the students are African American, 13 percent are Hispanic, and 4 percent are Asian. Only one third are white. This mix did not happen accidentally. The college was started as a Presbyterian seminary in the last century for German immigrants, many of whom arrived at nearby Ellis Island. But the surrounding community changed, and new immigrants arrived—this time from nations to the south and west. The college chose to change as well.

College officials do more than simply recruit minority students, however. They have made diversity the centerpiece of its mission. "A conscious effort was made not just to change with the area, but to dedicate ourselves to the population we serve," says George Lynes, III, dean of admissions. The college works deliberately to increase the number of minority faculty; 19 percent of teachers are African American, for example. In addition, the curriculum tries to reflect different cultures and acknowledge different traditions. "All courses, including the physical sciences, are required to approach their disciplines from a multiracial, multicultural perspective," says Lynes.

This philosophy prepares students—of all races—for the future. "The reality of our society is that it is no longer a largely white community. . . . We're preparing kids for the kind of world we live in," he says.

Most colleges are less heterogeneous. But diversity should be a goal for every institution. When examining an institution, look for a commitment to minority students and, of special importance, find out how the curriculum and faculty reflect changes taking place in America as a whole.

Are different cultures and traditions studied in the classroom and celebrated across campus?

International Students Promote Global Awareness

Diversity also requires an international perspective. A good college will enroll students from around the world, and it will reflect global concerns in the curriculum and through guest lectures, cultural presentations, festivals, and more. America is the favorite destination for international students. However, foreign students too often have little impact on most campuses. While a college or university will boast that it attracts learners from many countries, these students are usually not asked to contribute their knowledge and experiences to the rest of the college community. At most institutions, they are a small, voiceless minority.

A commitment to international understanding, then, requires more than the presence of foreign students. Instead, these students should be encouraged to participate fully in campus activities. Find out not only the percentage of international students but also investigate what role they play on campus. Are they invited to make presentations and participate fully in campus life? Nearly half a million foreign students are currently enrolled in American higher education, but they make up only 3 percent or less of the student population at most colleges and universities. There are, however, a few institutions where the campus is a true multinational community.

At the American University of Paris in France, for example, students come from ninety different nations. Although the institution is fully accredited, teaches in English, and follows an American-style liberal arts curriculum, Americans reflect only one third of the population. In this setting, students of all nationalities learn to live and work as part of a global community. "If you take an international affairs class, and your professor is from Iran and half the students are from the Middle East, we're not going to have a lecture class, we're going to have a seminar," say David Richter, a 1988 graduate. "You have a lot of feelings coming from the heart. And that," he adds, "just makes a world of difference. Students walk out of class with a greater understanding of their subject, and a deeper understanding of each other."

Are student-run organizations an active part of campus life?

Extracurricular activities—from drama clubs to student government—are not just diversions. They help students develop new interests, get ready for a career, and learn important leadership skills.

Look at how students work together outside the classroom. Is there a wide range of student clubs? How many students volunteer on campus and in the community? Are there all-campus traditions that unite the community? What percentage of students participate? On any given day, students might, for example, be found writing stories for the campus newspaper, rehearsing for a new play, attending a political meeting, or volunteering for a social service agency. These types of activities bring an infectious spirit of energy and enthusiasm to a campus.

The Role of Student Government

Look, too, at student government. Is it taken seriously by students and administrators? Many student government organizations have little or no real authority, but some help shape the future of a college or university. At the University of North Carolina at Chapel Hill, for example, the student body president is a voting member of the board of trustees.

Marlboro College in Marlboro, Vermont, operates under a New England town meeting style of government. Each member—including all students—has equal say in college governance. Students also sit on committees responsible for faculty hiring, admissions, and curriculum decisions. "A Vermont college with Vermont values," its president explains in a *Boston Globe* article (June 4, 1995).

Without question, these experiences build real leadership skills. But a growing number of colleges and universities focus on leadership in other ways. The Leadership Development program at West Virginia State College, a historically black college in Institute, West Virginia, invites speakers from different professions to talk informally with students about their experiences as leaders. At Texas Christian University in Fort Worth, Texas, students may also work with leaders in their community, who act as advisers and role models. Similar programs are offered at Wartburg College in Waverly, Iowa, and Miami University in Oxford, Ohio.

Getting All Students Involved

Part-time and commuter students represent a special challenge for colleges. As a group, they have less free time and are less inclined to contribute to student life. A college with a large commuter student population may, if it's not careful, turn into little more than a parking lot with classrooms; all sense of community is lost.

A college cannot force students to participate in extracurricular activities, but many try to entice them back on campus. Day-care services and commuter student lounges are offered on some campuses. These and other facilities encourage nontraditional students to spend time on campus and find their own niche. If you are looking at colleges with a large commuter student population, find out how active this group is on campus. They can either support, or hinder, extracurricular life.

The Pros and Cons of Greek Life

Fraternities and sororities should also be investigated. They are an important part of many college and university communities and, at their best, build camaraderie among members and sponsor community service projects. Yet, on too many campuses, they almost completely define student social life and tend to divide, not unify, the campus. Acts of blatant racism, sexism, and uncontrolled brutality during initiation hazings have tarnished the image of some.

Fraternities and sororities are here to stay. However, we believe their role on campus should be carefully examined. Have any been cited for violations of alcohol and other campus policies? Do they dominate the college or university's social life? Do students who are not members feel left out? If the answer is yes, we recommend you look elsewhere. Some colleges have removed, or never allowed, fraternities and sororities on their campuses.

Concern About Big-Time Athletics

Athletics is another contentious issue in higher education. A football or basketball team—especially a winning team—can bring an institution together. Intramural sports and fitness programs, especially, encourage the whole campus community to participate and become active. But big-time athletics is, at best, a mixed blessing. For most of this century, critics have lamented the attention given intercollegiate athletics and the ethical breaches that too often result. A 1929 Carnegie Foundation report, *American College Athletics*, found it to be both corrupt and corrupting: "More than any other force [athletics have] tended to distort the values of college life," it said.

In recent years, steps have been taken on some campuses to improve reputations tarnished by recruiting and other scandals. But it is still important to remember that a university is not a "good school" simply because it is an athletic powerhouse.

In the end, a college must be judged not just by the amount or variety of student activity. Instead, ask one final question: Does the institution act like a real community? More than a collection of learners, with each pursuing separate academic, political, and social interests, a college or university should build a shared identity. There must be traditions and activities pursued across campus that reinforce the best values of American society. Is the spirit of this search felt as well?

In America there is concern that society is dangerously divided along myriad faultlines that reinforce stereotypes and prejudices. The nation must search for and celebrate those things that hold us together as Americans and citizens of the world. Robert Bellah eloquently describes this urgent task in his book *Habits of the Heart:*

> If we are not entirely a mass of interchangeable fragments within an aggregate, if we are in part qualitatively distinct members of a whole, it is because there are still operating among us, with whatever difficulties, traditions that tell about the nature of society, and about who we are as a people.

Colleges and universities have a special responsibility to affirm these essential connections by the climates they foster on their respective campuses.

The Key Questions to Ask

Is the campus a true community? Here are a few questions that help give you the answer.

1. Is the campus safe?
- Does the college or university make its crime statistics available to prospective students?
- Does the institution help ensure safety through campus police, escort services, adequate lighting, and other strategies?
- How safe do current students feel? Are they satisfied with campus security?
- Is the code of conduct respected by students, staff, and faculty? How has it made the campus a safer, more respectful community?

2. Are cultural opportunities offered?
- Does the college or university host a wide variety of speakers, artists, and performers?

3. Are residence halls a place to live and to learn?
- Are social and cultural events regularly held in residence halls?
- Are faculty regularly invited to meet with students in residence halls?
- Is hall life guided by clear rules of behavior?
- Are resident counselors trained for the responsibilities they are given and supervised by professional staff?

4. **Is diversity respected and celebrated?**

- Does the student body reflect the growing diversity of America?
- Are different cultures and values reflected in the curriculum and celebrated across the campus?
- Is an international perspective emphasized?

5. **Are student organizations an active part of campus life?**

- Are there a rich variety of student clubs and extracurricular activities?
- Is student government a respected part of college life? Do students help shape the future of the institution?
- Are there all-campus traditions uniting the community?
- How many students actively participate in government and other student organizations?

9

Services for Students

For years, "student services"—everything from the health center to the career planning office—has been a nearly invisible part of higher education. But on many campuses, these valuable programs are emerging from the shadows, taking a larger and more active role.

The health center, for example, may do much more than treat illness. Today, many now focus on wellness through seminars and health fairs that promote exercise, nutrition, and other good habits. The career center is more than a job bulletin board ignored by all but a few seniors. Instead, many centers work with students during all four or more years of study, helping them learn about their career options. Likewise, academic tutoring and psychological counseling also reach out to serve more people.

Although each meets a distinct need, collectively these programs form a kind of safety net, helping students make the transition to adult life, graduate from college, and be ready for the future. At a good college, these services also teach skills and habits that encourage success long after graduation.

The Real World

Students often call life beyond campus "the real world," as if college is isolated from outside pressures and responsibilities. But, more than ever before, the real world intrudes on even the most bucolic campus: Students struggle to meet their many responsibilities; they worry about finding a career after graduation; and, to an alarming degree, they suffer both physically and emotionally from the hectic pace of college life. All this generates stress and—for some—moments of true crisis.

Colleges and universities respond with services that help students stay healthy and succeed academically. Tutors are available for students baffled by a professor's assignment. Counseling centers attend to emotional needs. Health centers treat illness and may focus on health education. Career centers are available for those hunting for a job and, often, arrange valuable work-related internships. These programs are found, in some form, on nearly every campus. They are a necessary part of every college's infrastructure. But not all are the same. On some campuses, these services touch the lives of nearly all students and build a stronger and healthier community.

When made a priority, a creative, well-supported package of supportive services may mean the difference between academic success and failure. The best programs reach out to all students, teaching them the skills they need to stay healthy, cope with stress, and discover a rewarding career. Every institution must make some effort to help each student overcome the barriers—academic, physical, and emotional—he or she may face while enrolled.

Does the college or university tutor students needing extra academic support?

How do the colleges and universities that you are considering reach out to students who need help academically? Are tutors available to help students learn study skills and complete difficult assignments?

Often, students learn to be successful scholars by trial and error. Although academic success requires good study habits, wise use of free time, and the ability to take tests, these and other essential skills are often discovered, not taught.

Many colleges and universities, however, sponsor academic support centers where students can learn strategies for success. The best programs are open to all students during most hours of the day and are staffed by professional advisers and trained student tutors. Students typically go to an academic support center when they are having trouble with a particular class. Maybe they can't solve a math problem or don't understand a scientific concept. Tutors sit down with them to help solve their problem and get them back on track.

But many programs do more. They also help identify deeper problems that students may be having academically. Students will then leave with more than an answer; they may learn study skills that will help them in all classes.

Teaching Study Skills

According to Ken Kirkpatrick, director of the Academic Resource Center at DePauw University in Greencastle, Indiana, most students come in because they are stumped by an assignment. "Almost 90 percent come and identify themselves as needing help with just one problem," he says. But in nearly every instance, study skills are to blame. For example, students having trouble in chemistry often fail to carefully read test questions. "So we talk to them about reading techniques, identifying key words and terms in a question, and identifying, before they start, what the answer should be," Kirkpatrick says.

Many other universities offer similar programs. The University of Massachusetts Lowell, for example, sponsors an active peer tutoring program where students find help with class assignments and can participate in exam review sessions. Tutors are fellow students who have been recommended by professors and formally trained for their job. The program at the University of Massachusetts is a drop-in center; appointments are not necessary, and all students are served. According to Sheila Riley-Callahan, director of academic services, it is especially popular with freshmen and sophomores.

Offering Extra Help

These and other programs often provide extra assistance to students in especially difficult classes. At DePauw University, Ken Kirkpatrick identifies courses where students are more likely to fail. He then attends class with students and even takes the tests. "I'm then able to prepare test-taking workshops specifically on that course rather than just giving students some general stuff on multiple-choice testing," he says.

California Polytechnic State University, San Luis Obispo, offers workshops to support students in key math courses. This intensive program meets 4 hours a week, and participating students earn academic credit. Although most students who attend workshops are considered at risk academically, they actually outperform their classmates, according to student academic services director Armando Pezo-Silva.

Do the colleges and universities that you are considering have a formal academic resource center, or similar program where students can go for tutoring? Although large universities are more likely to offer the most comprehensive programs, small colleges may sponsor volunteer tutoring services and build a less formal, but still effective, academic support network. Equally important, are these services user friendly? Is the center conveniently located and open in the evening, when students are most likely to be studying and need a question answered?

For example, Indiana University Bloomington recently put an academic support center inside one of its residence halls. Open from 8 a.m. to midnight, students can find help in writing, math, study skills, and test taking at almost any hour. "It's very accessible at a place where students study and at times when it's most helpful," says associate dean Michael Morgan.

Centers Support Faculty

These programs are not meant to replace the important faculty-student relationship. However, colleges and universities acknowledge that professors—especially those teaching large classes—do not always have the time to meet with all students. In addition, tutors may be less threatening to students.

Sheila Riley-Callahan says her program was at first resented by some professors. "Faculty felt students should come to them [rather than go to the center]," she recalls. But most now understand that the program offers students something extra. It's a place for those who need more extensive help or are, perhaps, intimidated by their professors. "When they come here it's like neutral ground," she says.

Does the college or university emphasize student health?

On most campuses, the old-fashioned "infirmary" is now being updated with a campuswide emphasis on wellness. Innovative colleges and universities offer a range of programs that encourage exercise, good nutrition, and healthy lifestyles.

Nearly all colleges and universities have a student health center. At a small institution, it may be little more than a room with a nurse and occasional visits from a doctor. At some large universities, it may look and feel more like a hospital. The health center at the University of Georgia in Athens, for example, employs thirteen full-time physicians, a staff of specialists and clinicians, and operates a pharmacy. It is even able to serve students with chronic diseases such as diabetes and cancer.

Health centers are an important service. But even the best-equipped infirmary should be just one part of a larger campuswide emphasis on health education. In the dining room, gym, and residence hall, students should be encouraged to maintain good health.

Americans are regularly reminded that good health depends on good habits and that stress can lead to illness. If this is true, then college students arrive on campus already at risk. The pressure to adapt to a new home and succeed academically is emotionally and physically exhausting. Exercise and good nutrition may be neglected; alcohol and drugs may be a temptation. Too many students look and feel sick, even when they are not ill.

"College is one of the most stressful times. [Students] don't eat well, they don't sleep well, and they don't take care of themselves," says Sue Heimann, dean of students at Ashland University in Ohio. They also have little understanding of their own physical limitations. "You're dealing with an age group that thinks they're invincible and invulnerable," she explains. It's a potent combination. Many students ignore warnings and push their bodies too far.

A Focus on Prevention

In response, Heiman's university offers a comprehensive program that includes health-care and wellness education. Along with a student health center, Ashland trains peer educators who make presentations to students on alcohol use, contraception, stress, eating disorders, and other issues important to college students. The university also sponsors a campuswide health fair every two years. Students can have their blood pressure taken, cholesterol tested, and learn about university and community programs that promote physical and emotional health. Students are being taught to take responsibility for their health—and become wise consumers of health care. The health center takes the time to explain medical procedures to student patients and to discuss the side effects of prescription medicine. "We want them to leave the university knowing that when they are at a physician's office, they should ask questions and know that they are paying for answers," says Heimann.

Other colleges and universities have equally innovative services. Southern Illinois University at Carbondale has programs devoted to stress management, nutrition, alcohol, and drug prevention. Framingham State College in Framingham, Massachusetts, teaches first aid and CPR classes as part of its health program. East Stroudsburg University of Pennsylvania has a Relaxation Room where students can sit in comfortable chairs, listen to music, and escape, at least briefly, the pressures of college life.

Do the colleges and universities that you are considering treat and help prevent illness? Is health education a formal part of the health center's mission? Where and how is this taught? Ask students what they think about these and similar programs offered on campus.

Nutrition Matters, Too

Nutrition should also be a priority. The college dining hall is the butt of a thousand jokes—many of them well deserved. But, acknowledging the limitations of institutional food, every college should offer a variety of healthy alternatives and give students the nutrition information they need when making their selections. The University of Georgia, for example, lists the calorie and fat content of its dishes. It also offers brochures, lectures, and classes on eating disorders, dieting, and vegetarianism.

Of course, good food is the best incentive. Take a look at dining hall fare. Are the healthy alternatives as attractive and appealing as, say, the donuts and desserts?

Does the college or university offer psychological counseling services?

Every college must help students complete the transition to college and adult life. Professional counselors should help students suffering from all the emotional ailments found on nearly every modern college campus.

How stressful is college? According to one often-cited study, the start of formal higher education is more nerve-racking than marriage, divorce, or a jail sentence. In a list of 100 different life changes, only death of a spouse, child, or other close relation ranked higher.

This doesn't surprise Jonathan Kandell from the University of Maryland College Park counseling center. "For one thing," he dryly notes, "jail is a much more structured environment. "You know what you're supposed to do. And if you don't do it you know what the consequences are." College, in contrast, offers almost overwhelming freedom. Especially for students leaving home for the first time, every day presents a new challenge. "It's a very different experience," Kandell says. "It's the first time students have the freedom to make decisions. They don't have to go to class if they don't want to. There's no one looking over their shoulder." What's right? What are the consequences? The answers are not always obvious.

For Students, an Uncertain Future

And the pressures are growing more intense. Counseling offices are seeing a greater number of students in distress. "The trend has been to more cases, and more severe cases," Kandell says, both on his campus and nationwide.

Students are worried—about money, the future, their ability to succeed academically. They also bring more problems with them to school, reflecting the stress of modern life and greater diversity in the college population. Older students must juggle school with family and work responsibilities, for example. Minorities must overcome racial and cultural barriers. Many students enter academically unprepared. "A lot of students are coming in with recurring depression that they bring from elsewhere, with suicide stuff in their heads, with issues of alcohol, with incest, date rape," says Karyl Lyne, director of student academic services at Eastern New Mexico University in Portales. "All those things affect academic performance."

The Counselor's Role

In response, many colleges and universities offer counselors, or full-fledged counseling centers, where students can find professional and confidential help with emotional problems. Typically, they offer one-on-one sessions for students with depression, anxiety, problems with personal relationships, eating disorders—"a whole variety of things," says Jonathan Kandell.

Do the schools that you are considering meet this minimum requirement? Especially important: Are there enough counselors to serve students seeking this kind of help? Bob Gallagher, director of the counseling center at the University of Pittsburgh in Pittsburgh, Pennsylvania, says there should be one counselor for every thousand students. Many schools—especially large universities—fall short, he acknowledges. But a ratio of one counselor per 3,000 students or higher should be a clear warning sign, he explains. Also ask if the counseling center is accredited and if the staff has the credentials for the work they do.

Be sure, too, that counselors are employees of the college or university. Although the practice is still rare, some institutions are cutting costs by paying outside contractors to manage counseling services. Gallagher says these firms do not always understand the emotional needs of students. In some cases, they may not even work on campus.

Many colleges offer even more by actively reaching out to students who are considered at risk or may need more support. Some institutions have support groups that address addiction or sexual assault, for example. Eastern New Mexico University sponsors student-run support programs for Hispanic, Native American, African-American, and nontraditional students.

Is the counseling program supported by faculty? Professors are no longer expected to oversee the emotional and moral development of their students, but they are often the first to see signs of distress. Explains Karyl Lyne: "We miss the boat as higher educators when we don't pay attention to warning signals in class; when, for instance, we have a perfectly wonderful student who suddenly quits coming to class. Or is in class—but is not really there. Those are signals of more than just academic problems."

To be effective, a counseling program needs understanding and support from the faculty. How are teachers taught about the work of counselors and encouraged to refer students in need? Emotional health is no less important than physical health and deserves the same level of concern and attention from all members of the college community.

Does the college or university help students find a career?

Colleges and universities should help students make the transition to work. Career centers must help students explore their interests, learn about different careers, and, ultimately, find the job that meets their needs.

Colleges prepare students for work, but the transition from classroom to career is often difficult. Once again, students are starting over, asking new questions: How do I find a job? What do I say in an interview? What does a good résumé look like? Many learn too late unwelcome facts about their chosen profession: No jobs are available, the pay is too low, or the work is unpleasant. "If only I had known!" is often the new graduate's cry of lament.

Colleges and universities typically offer a career center. There, students—especially seniors—may learn about job openings or find help writing their résumé. For many students, it's their last stop before graduation. A number of career centers, however, are taking a more active role, emphasizing career planning, not just placement. They are sponsoring programs that reach out to students who are only beginning to think about their career interests.

At Flagler College in St. Augustine, Florida, for example, all students begin preparing for work as soon as they arrive on campus by learning about careers and starting to build marketable skills.

Exploring Career Interests

In the freshman year, the career center at Flagler helps students explore their options: What are their interests? What careers satisfy these interests? Are jobs available? What kind of pay should they expect? This brief session doesn't answer every question, but it does encourage students to start thinking about the future, says Helen Amato, Flagler College's career planning officer.

In the sophomore year, all students write their first résumé. Most of these résumés are weak; few students have skills that will entice an employer. But Amato accentuates the positive. With two years of college left, she says, they have time to fill in the gaps. Instead of delivering pizzas during the summer, for example, they are encouraged to find a job or internship related to their career interest.

By the junior year, one-on-one meetings help students begin the transition to work. They are encouraged to learn about the latest trends in their future profession by reading trade journals. Information-gathering interviews are recommended to students who have not yet made a career choice. This process continues into the senior year, when students complete a final résumé.

Finding a Job

This process helps make the long-anticipated leap from college to work. Students, it is hoped, leave with a better understanding of their career choices and make a better impression when they approach potential employers. Amato cautions, however, that her office cannot do everything. "Occasionally I'll get a cock robin who comes through my door and says, 'Now, where are you going to get me a job?' Nobody in career services gets anybody a job," she answers. "All we do is help you prepare yourself for an aggressive, professional job search. Getting a job—networking, getting interviewed—is your job."

The program at Flagler College is unusual because it is mandatory, but other colleges and universities across the country now offer a similar range of services. Professional career planning staff members help students learn about career options. In some cases, these offices are responsible for all internships offered to students.

An even more recent trend in higher education is to offer career training to alumni. Several colleges and universities have programs for former students searching for a new job, extending support to students long after graduation. Clients meet with counselors, participate in workshops, and have their résumés placed in a database.

How do the colleges or universities that you are considering help students prepare for life after school? Does career planning start early? How do students learn about the different job options? How are students prepared to find a good job and get hired? Finally, what percentage of students use the services of a career center? Does the center reach out to students by, for example, making presentations to classes?

Career preparation is not the only goal of undergraduate education. Students should not feel compelled to spend every waking hour getting ready for a job. College should also be a time to explore new interests and gain new experiences. On the other hand, higher education has, in the past, let students graduate with little information about their career choices. The programs at Flagler College and elsewhere help students enter the workplace with greater confidence.

Putting the Pieces Together

We have described different ways a college or university can help its students. Each meets a specific need. But, in the end, it is difficult to separate one from the other. The physical, emotional, and academic are connected. Some institutions are, therefore, trying to eliminate the barriers dividing one kind of support program from the other. At these schools, students have one-stop shopping for everything from math tutoring to résumé writing.

This philosophy is reflected at Eastern New Mexico University in Portales, where most services are located together in a single building on the edge of campus. The Student Academic Services building provides counseling and tutoring, study skills courses, career placement, and more in offices surrounding a sunny atrium. In one office, a peer tutor is helping a student solve a math problem. Down the hall, a senior is planning a job search at the career center. On another floor, a graduate psychology student is counseling a freshman with depression. A student health center, located elsewhere, completes this comprehensive package of services that nearly every student uses at least once and that many use repeatedly.

Putting most of these services under one roof reflects a belief that academic and emotional needs are intertwined and have a direct effect on a student's ability to succeed in and out of the classroom. For example, a student frustrated by poor grades may come in seeking a tutor but, in the end, may benefit from other types of counseling. Referrals are easily made. "It's my belief that a student who is experiencing academic difficulty is probably experiencing a variety of other difficulties as well," says Karyl Lyne. Poor grades are often the symptom, not the problem, she explains.

Most institutions do not put all their services under one roof; at a small college, especially, this may not be necessary. But the program at Eastern New Mexico University is an important reminder that students' success requires individual support and attention. When the focus is on the whole student, a strong network of support is created that, in some way, benefits all.

The Key Questions To Ask

Nearly all colleges and universities offer a program of student support services. To identify the best, ask the following questions.

1. Is academic tutoring offered?
- Is the tutoring center conveniently located on campus?
- Students study at all hours. Is the center open in evenings—even on weekends?
- Is the center staffed by professional tutors? Are student tutors formally trained?
- Does the center help students learn more effectively by, for example, teaching study skills, time management, and test-taking strategies?

2. Is student health a priority?
- Is health education a formal part of the student health center's mission?
- How is this taught? For example, are presentations made to students in residence halls, classes, or health fairs?
- Are students taught about good nutrition—and offered a selection of healthy alternatives in the dining hall?

3. Are psychological counseling services a priority?
- Are there enough counselors to serve all students in need? Professionals recommend no less than one for every thousand students.

- Are these counselors specialists in the needs of students? Are they employees of the college who work on campus?
- Are special programs or support groups offered for minority students? Nontraditional students?
- Do faculty members work with counselors, helping to identify students who show signs of distress?

4. What role does the career center play?

- Does it focus on career planning during all four or more years of study?
- Does it help students find internships and other work-related experiences?
- What percentage of students use its services? How does it reach out to the campus community and encourage greater student participation?

Measuring the Outcomes

I s college worth the investment? Educators say yes. But parents, students, and many others now want proof. More than ever, Americans are asking how higher education makes a difference. Do graduates get better jobs? Do they earn more money? As college costs climb, these questions are becoming more commonplace.

The focus is on what educators call the *outcomes* of higher education. It is no longer enough to say students are educated—and better prepared for life—just because they went to college. Instead, colleges and universities now examine what all students learn and track their progress after they leave. Students may be asked to complete standardized tests, compile portfolios of their work, or answer surveys.

But, at its best, assessment is also an opportunity for students. It should be a time for *self*-examination—an opportunity to reflect on all they have learned, see how the parts fit together, and prepare for life after college.

In this final chapter, we describe how colleges encourage this kind of reflection through senior seminars, theses, and colloquia—classes and projects that reveal the full value and richness of undergraduate education.

Putting the Pieces Together

Between the first and last day of college, most students have spent at least four years on campus. They have completed dozens of courses and countless quizzes, tests, papers, and oral reports. Many have traveled overseas, finished an internship, or helped run student government. Now all requirements have been met and a diploma is due.

But before students don cap and gown, one final question must be asked: What have they learned?

This simple question is, perhaps, the hardest yet. Of course, it is possible to describe the individual pieces of a college education; students can list the classes taken and some of the facts they learned. But it is much harder to put these pieces together and examine the meaning and impact of the whole college experience.

This question goes to the heart of a liberal arts education. In the end, all students should leave with not just the skills needed to earn a living, but also the insight required to solve problems, make wise decisions, and advance the common good. Ultimately, the knowledge gained in the classroom and across campus must guide students throughout a lifetime, both as workers and citizens. If this higher purpose is not achieved, then students have ultimately gained little more than a sack full of academic credits.

In this chapter, we describe how colleges and universities ask students to engage in this kind of reflection and to show that the many pieces of their education add up to a coherent whole. In their final months of study, for example, seniors may complete a comprehensive paper or take part in a senior seminar where social and ethical issues are discussed—using insights gleaned from all their classes and extracurricular experiences. We also describe how a good school tracks student progress after graduation. Alumni surveys find out if former students are satisfied with their careers and have benefitted in other important, if less tangible, ways. These insights will help refine the curriculum, services, and even the mission of the institution. In this way, students become partners in education reform.

Do all students complete a senior seminar and senior paper?

All graduating students should be able to communicate clearly and apply what they have learned to real-world problems. Senior-year seminars and papers are opportunities for students to demonstrate their competency in these areas by synthesizing all aspects of their education.

More than anything else, undergraduate education is about the search for connections—within the curriculum and to the world beyond. The whole college experience, at its best, is a seamless web, with each part—general education, the major, the extracurricular—supporting the other. But how, in the end, are these parts brought together? And how do students show they understand—and can apply to their own lives—the larger goals of higher education?

Many colleges and universities set aside time in the senior year for classes, colloquia, and special projects that encourage this kind of reflection. Through senior seminars, papers, and other projects, students are asked to demonstrate that they are leaving college with a capacity to think clearly and to organize and communicate ideas in an effective, integrative way.

Senior Seminars Examine the Big Picture

In senior seminars—also called "capstone" courses— students typically explore significant social or political issues in their last year of study, applying what they have learned to larger problems.

The University of Wisconsin–Green Bay, for example, offers a variety of senior seminars, each organized around a significant intellectual or social problem. All are taught as small discussion and writing-intensive classes and include students from a wide range of majors. According to Irene Kiefer, executive director of university communication, this allows students to "extend, apply, and integrate knowledge." For example, "The science student will bring a totally different perspective than someone who has been in the business program." Faculty members work hard to include these different views, she says.

At Bradford College in Bradford, Massachusetts, the senior seminar is a time for students to apply what they have learned to real-life ethical and moral issues. Management students, for example, discourse on business ethics. They use writing and critical thinking skills first introduced in freshman English classes as they research and publicly defend their positions. They may refer back to information taught in courses ranging from philosophy to science. They think about the practical lessons they learned through internships and off-campus study. "On and on, you can look down the curriculum and ask students, 'Those were all great as individual courses, but how do they come together?'" says Howard Brown, chair of the management division.

Ideally, the colleges and universities that you are considering make senior seminars a required part of each student's education. Students should be expected to demonstrate their ability to write clearly and apply theoretical knowledge to practical problems.

Senior Projects as a Bridge to Work

The senior project is the culmination of college learning—the undergraduate equivalent of a master's thesis. Indeed, at many colleges and universities, it is called the senior thesis and is expected to be a piece of original research (see chapter 5 for more about student research).

At other colleges, the senior project can take many different shapes. For example, at Bradford College, it may be a dance performance, art exhibit, or detailed business plan, depending on the student's major. In many cases, these projects help students make the transition to their first career. William Dunfey, Bradford College's dean of admissions, explains, "The goal in the student's senior year, especially, is to ease from collegiate education to employment. The senior project is a major undertaking that could be a bridge to the real world."

For example, one management student met the requirement—and prepared for her future—by studying how to start an art supply business, says Howard Brown. A Vietnamese student learned how to market insurance to the Vietnamese community in Boston. Other students presented their senior projects to potential employers as a tangible demonstration of their ability. In Howard Brown's management division, most documents are between 50 and 100 pages, reflecting the depth of research and analysis required.

The final requirement is a public presentation of the project. Within the management division, students have 20 minutes to describe their findings and respond to questions from faculty, outside evaluators, students, and other members of the college community. The senior project is an important part of Bradford College's core curriculum and also plays a part in the assessment process. By completing independent research or a creative project, students are asked to demonstrate the full breadth of their knowledge. This, in turn, helps educators serve students even better. By looking for trends in student work, a college or university can identify weaknesses in the curriculum and make improvements.

At the University of South Carolina–Aiken, new courses have been added and existing courses changed after faculty identified weaknesses in the senior projects completed by their students. This kind of formal institutional assessment happens behind the scenes but is another way colleges and universities are becoming more accountable.

Are senior projects required for graduation at the schools you are considering? How are students guided through the research process? Do students formally present their findings to the college community? For example, some colleges sponsor an all-college colloquium where projects are presented and discussed.

Are student opinions part of assessment?

Graduates have experienced their college in action. They know what works and what doesn't. A good college or university will therefore ask students to describe their college experience and use the findings to make improvements.

All colleges and universities want their graduates to be successful. A school's credibility grows when their students find good jobs or are admitted to prestigious graduate schools. Many colleges now track student progress after graduation, eager to learn how they are doing. They survey graduates to find out how many work, how much they earn, and how many go back to school for more education.

Many colleges use this data when recruiting new students. Johnson & Wales University in Providence, Rhode Island, which offers degrees in food service and hospitality from five campuses across the country, reports that 98 percent of graduates find jobs within sixty days. The viewbook of Kalamazoo College, in Kalamazoo, Michigan, says between 85 and 95 percent of its graduates who applied to law and medical school in recent years were admitted. Fort Lewis College in Durango, Colorado, found that about half of its alumni describe their job level as "professional" or "upper management." The message to potential students is: "Our graduates are successful—you will be too."

This kind of tracking can serve another purpose as well. In addition to highlighting strengths, it can discover weaknesses and—most important—lead to improvement. In this way, student opinion becomes an important part of the assessment process and ultimately creates an even stronger institution.

When considering a college or university, find out if all graduates complete formal surveys that ask questions about all aspects of their college experience. These surveys should be completed soon after graduation. Follow-up surveys should be completed in later years. Especially important, find out how results from these surveys are used. Have changes been made to the curriculum, campus activities, or student services in response to insights gleaned from alumni comments?

Earlham College in Richmond, Indiana, sends out surveys one, five, and ten years after graduation. The one-year survey asks students if their undergraduate education helped them in their work or graduate program. Later surveys ask students to reflect more deeply on their experiences in college and the values it taught: How do they feel about their major? The financial aid office? The social life? Do they feel the college prepared them professionally? Are they active in political and social issues? These and dozens of additional questions search for meaningful insights about the institution and its lasting influence on those who attend.

What has Earlham College found in its survey results? Graduates said good things about the college, but there was room for improvement. For example, the career services office received relatively low marks from students responding to recent five- and ten-year surveys. "I could have used some exposure to internships and practicum, etc.," one student wrote, "but I, like a lot of students, was too lazy to find the career center and pursue this on my own." In response, Wendy Seligmann, the current director of career services, took action. She now makes presentations to classes, telling students about her office and especially about the value of internships. In one recent class, all students were required to identify ten internships—and actually apply to one. This is one example of how student surveys can make a lasting impact on their schools.

Of course, these surveys also provide insight for prospective students. In addition to the pieces of data featured in viewbooks, an institution should be willing to share the full findings of its research. At Earlham College, Seligmann says that survey data are available to all prospective students through her office.

Other colleges and universities collect similar data in other ways. They conduct formal exit interviews, examine portfolios of student work, and even interview employers. In each, educators come to better understand the needs of students, the impact of higher education, and the strengths of their institutions. At its best, however, assessment focuses on the larger goals of higher education, not just data about student employment, income, or graduate study.

Ready for the Future

Now, at last, students are ready for graduation. They leave, certainly, with a credential and a set of skills that prepare them for a career or further study. But at a college of quality, they have gained even more.

First, students leave with mastery of the English language. Freshman seminars, writing-intensive classes, senior research, and more have built proficiency in the most essential of all human skills. More than minimally competent, they have learned to make language a powerful tool. Next, through a core curriculum and enriched major, students leave with essential skills, as well as an ability to find connections across the disciplines and to life beyond campus. From the freshman to the senior year, students are guided through a logical sequence of courses that add up to a coherent whole.

In addition, students have learned to take charge of their own education. They are active participants in classroom discussions and collaborate with other students on common projects. They may create independent study projects and participate in research and can find and apply information contained in books, periodicals, and computers. The skills and confidence taught in college help them make the transition to work with greater ease and prepare them for a lifetime of learning.

Finally, students are ready to contribute to society. A focus on service reminds students that we all have a responsibility to build strong caring communities. Leadership skills are nurtured through student government and student organizations. A campus that reflects—and celebrates—America's rich ethnic diversity prepares students for changes taking place in the nation.

Senior seminars and research papers are an opportunity to put all these pieces together. But at the best colleges and universities, it is a process that began on the first day of new student orientation and continued in each class, through each term.

The Key Questions to Ask

College must be more than the sum of its parts. At a college or university of quality, students reflect on what they have learned through senior seminars and senior projects. Alumni surveys are used to create an even stronger institution for future generations of learners.

1. **Do all students complete a senior seminar and senior project?**
   - Do these "capstone" experiences encourage students to apply all they have learned in college—through general education, the major, and extracurricular work?
   - Are senior papers and projects formally presented to the college community?

2. **Do alumni surveys help improve the quality of the college or university?**
   - How often are alumni surveyed? How are responses used to improve the quality of the institution? Are college officials able to give specific examples?
   - Are the full results of recent alumni surveys available to prospective students?

Checklist of Key Questions to Ask Colleges

These questions, which appear at the end of the appropriate chapters, are gathered here in one comprehensive checklist to provide you with a summary of the ten key criteria of quality in a college education. Use it to guide you as you evaluate schools from guides and viewbooks, visit campuses, and speak with admissions officers, students, faculty members, and college alumni.

Chapter 1: Getting Ready for College

Transition and orientation programs set the tone for college learning. Carefully investigate how the colleges and universities you consider support new students.

1. **Does the college or university give you the information you need to make the right choice?**

   - Does it describe the specific requirements for admission—such as the range of acceptable test scores or minimum GPA?
   - Does it report retention rates and give data showing where students go after graduation? For example, what percentage find work? What percentage continue their education?
   - Does the institution's mission statement specifically talk about the importance of undergraduate education?
   - Do admissions staff members present the college or university honestly and answer questions fully?
   - Are you encouraged to wander around campus and visit informally with students, staff, and faculty?

2. **Does the college or university provide an orientation program?**

- Is it mandatory and free? If not, what percentage of students participate and what is the cost?
- Does it offer an introduction to both social and academic life? For example, do students take part in mini-classes or seminars? Do students formally meet with advisers and faculty?
- Does it build a sense of community by stressing campus traditions and values? Some colleges ask new students to take part in service learning projects. Others examine the issue of diversity.
- Are special orientation programs offered for older students, students with disabilities, or others with special needs?
- Do all members of the college community participate in orientation—including the president, faculty, and students?

3. **Does the college or university continue to support students during their first year of study through freshman seminars or college life classes?**

- Are they optional or required?
- Do they integrate living and learning? If not, how do they help students become an active part of the college community?

Chapter 2:
Clear Writing, Clear Thinking

How is language emphasized at the colleges and universities you are considering? All say they make language a priority. But all have different expectations. Some merely "encourage'' faculty to devise writing assignments. But others have specific writing and speaking requirements.

1. **Are writing, speaking, and critical thinking taught during the first year of study?**
   - Are one or more English composition courses required? Alternately, are these skills formally developed in a freshman seminar or similar course?

2. **Is language emphasized in all classes, during all four or more years of study?**
   - Are writing-intensive classes offered? How many are required for graduation?
   - Is writing a part of most—perhaps all—courses?

3. **Are trained tutors, or the resources of a writing center, available to students needing help?**
   - What services do they offer?
   - How accessible are they to students?
   - Are faculty members formally helped in their efforts to make writing a part of their courses?

4. **Are placement testing and remediation offered for students lacking college-level reading and writing skills?**

Chapter 3:
A Curriculum with Coherence

Give special consideration to colleges that make general education an important part of the undergraduate curriculum. It is the most effective way to teach general education and is also a clear sign that the college or university makes undergraduate education a priority.

1. **Is general education a priority?**
   - Does the college or university offer a core curriculum (a sequence of required courses) or a carefully developed set of distribution requirements? If distribution requirements are used, students should pick from a limited list of classes that, preferably, have been created just for the general education program.
   - How many general education courses are listed in the institution's course catalog? Do the courses appear connected to each other? Avoid colleges offering a long list of optional classes that are disconnected from each other and the rest of the curriculum.
   - Does the institution limit how many credits students may take in their majors?
   - Does the institution discourage students from completing double majors?

2. **Is general education supported through campuswide activities or off-campus travel?**
   - Are lectures, convocations, festivals, or other activities offered that directly support what is taught in the general education curriculum?
   - Travel to museums, cultural events—or even other countries—extend general education into the community and around the world. What opportunities does the college or university offer students?

3. **Does the college or university offer an "enriched" major?**
   - Does each major, even the most specialized, examine its field's historical, social, and ethical implications?

- Does general education support the major? For example, are required core courses taught during all years of study?

Chapter 4: Finding the Best Teachers

Within every college or university, the quality of teaching varies. But it is possible to identify institutions that try to support good teaching and make good teachers even better.

1. Who teaches?
- Is teaching skill evaluated when new faculty members are hired? For example, are candidates asked to teach a class or otherwise prove their skill in the classroom?
- Are undergraduate classes taught primarily by full-time faculty?
- Are teaching assistants formally trained and supervised as they learn the art of instruction?

2. Is good teaching rewarded?
- Is teaching ability seriously evaluated when tenure is being decided? Have faculty members been denied tenure for poor teaching ability?
- Are annual teaching awards given? How many? Is there a monetary award?

3. Who teaches the teachers?
- Are faculty members who receive teaching awards expected to mentor other faculty?
- Are grants available to faculty who wish to develop new courses or learn about new teaching methods?
- Does the college or university support a center for instructional improvement?

4. How are teachers evaluated?

- Are students asked to evaluate every class?
- Are these evaluations considered for tenure and promotion?
- Are faculty members also expected to evaluate the teaching performance of their colleagues—and help make improvements? Does this peer review continue throughout a professor's full career?

Chapter 5: The Creative Classroom

Do the colleges and universities you are considering make active learning a priority? These questions will help you find a school that brings creativity to the classoom.

1. Do teachers know their students?

- What is the average undergraduate class size?
- What are the largest and smallest classes taught? Specifically, how big is the largest required general education class?
- If large lecture classes are offered, are they accompanied by small discussion sections?
- How does your institution encourage informal interaction among faculty and students?

2. Do students participate in class?

- Are even first-year and introductory classes taught as seminars where students carry on discussions?
- Do students regularly work in small groups? Are they encouraged to collaborate on assignments and special projects? Is this a formal part of degree programs?

- Do students have the opportunity to become mentors, or even teachers, to other students? How extensive is the program? How are the students trained and supervised?

3. **Does learning take place outside the classroom?**
   - What opportunities exist for off-campus learning?
   - What percentage of students earn credit for work completed off campus?
   - How are students guided and advised as they complete off-campus studies?
   - Are telecommunications and other forms of electronic learning incorporated into classroom instruction? How many professors use the technology? Are they formally trained in its proper use?

4. **Do students take part in research?**
   - Are there opportunities for undergraduates to take part in faculty research? What role do they play? What percentage of students assist with faculty research?
   - Are all students expected to complete their own original research—such as a senior thesis—before graduation?

5. **Is service learning part of the curriculum?**
   - Do students earn credit for volunteer work?
   - What percentage of students participate in service learning?

Chapter 6: Resources for Learning

The library should be an essential part of every college and university campus. It should have a collection that meets the research needs of undergraduate students and a helpful, professional staff.

1. Does the library serve the needs of undergraduate students?

- What does the library spend annually on acquisitions and staff, per student? How does this compare with other institutions you are considering?
- Are students and staff happy with the library? Can they identify gaps in the collection?
- Does the library buy books recommended by students? Do they encourage student opinion in other ways?
- Do students have easy access to other college or university libraries?

2. Is the library connected to the information highway?

- Does the library offer computerized indexes and on-line databases for each of the major academic disciplines?
- Is the library connected to the Internet and World Wide Web?
- Are classrooms and dormitories also connected to a campuswide computer network?
- Is interlibrary loan free and easy to use?

3. Are students taught how to use library resources?

- Is library instruction a formal part of the undergraduate curriculum?
- Is the library staffed with reference librarians during all open hours?
- Are librarians considered faculty?

4. Does the college or university offer other resources for learning?

- Are botanical gardens, art museums, historical collections, or other artifacts part of the institution's collection?

- Are these resources used in undergraduate instruction?

Chapter 7: Extending the Campus

Colleges and universities are finding new ways to serve students. From internships to nontraditional degree programs, colleges have become more flexible and inclusive.

1. **Do students design their own majors?**
   - What percentage of students design their own programs of study?
   - How is the program supervised by faculty?

2. **Is credit awarded for independent study?**
   - Are students allowed—perhaps even encouraged—to earn credit through independent study projects?
   - Are internships also allowed?
   - Does the college help students find appropriate internships and supervise their progress?
   - Is a cooperative education program offered for students who want to combine college study with experience in the workforce?

3. **Where and when do students take classes?**
   - May students study part-time?
   - Are evening and/or weekend programs available for those needing more flexibility?
   - Is credit awarded for life experience? Is credit earned at other institutions honored?
   - Is it possible to earn a degree in less than four years?

4. **Is distance learning an option?**

- Is it possible to take courses through correspondence study?
- How are these courses or degree programs taught?
- Do students have easy access to professors and college services, even when they learn off campus?

Chapter 8: College Life

Is the campus a true community? Here are a few questions that help give you the answer.

1. Is the campus safe?
- Does the college or university make its crime statistics available to prospective students?
- Does the institution help ensure safety through campus police, escort services, adequate lighting, and other strategies?
- How safe do current students feel? Are they satisfied with campus security?
- Is the code of conduct respected by students, staff, and faculty? How has it made the campus a safer, more respectful community?

2. Are cultural opportunities offered?
- Does the college or university host a wide variety of speakers, artists, and performers?

3. Are residence halls places to both live and learn?
- Are social and cultural events regularly held in residence halls?
- Are faculty members regularly invited to meet with students in residence halls?
- Is hall life guided by clear rules of behavior?

- Are resident counselors trained for the responsibilities they are given and are they supervised by a professional staff?

4. Is diversity respected and celebrated?

- Does the student body reflect the growing diversity of America as a whole?
- Are different cultures and values reflected in the curriculum and celebrated across the campus?
- Is an international perspective also emphasized?

5. Are student organizations an active part of campus life?

- Are there a rich variety of student clubs and extracurricular activities?
- Is student government a respected part of college life? Do students help shape the future of the institution?
- Are there all-campus traditions uniting the community?
- How many students actively participate in government and other student organizations?

Chapter 9: Services for Students

Nearly all colleges and universities offer programs that help students academically and address their physical and emotional health. To identify the best, ask the following questions.

1. Is academic tutoring offered?

- Is the tutoring center conveniently located on campus?
- Students study at all hours. Is the center open in evenings—even nights and weekends?

- Is it staffed by professional tutors? Are student tutors formally trained?
- Does the center help students learn more effectively by, for example, teaching study skills, time management, and test-taking strategies?

2. Is student health a priority?

- Is health education a formal part of the student health center's mission?
- How is this taught? For example, are presentations made to students in residence halls, classes, or health fairs?
- Are students taught about good nutrition—and offered a selection of healthy alternatives in the dining hall?

3. Are psychological counseling services a priority?

- Are there enough counselors to serve all students in need? Professionals recommend no less than one for every thousand students.
- Are these counselors specialists in the needs of students? Are they employees of the college who work on campus?
- Are special programs or support groups offered for minority students? Nontraditional students?
- Do faculty members work with counselors, helping to identify students who show signs of distress?

4. What role does the career center play?

- Does it focus on career planning during all four or more years of study?
- Does it help students find internships and other work-related experiences?

- What percentage of students use its services? How does it reach out to the campus community and encourage greater student participation?

Chapter 10: Measuring the Outcomes

College must be more than the sum of its parts. At a college or university of quality, all students will reflect on all they have learned through senior seminars and senior projects. Alumni surveys will be used to create an even stronger institution for future generations of learners.

1. **Do all students complete a senior seminar and senior project?**
   - Do these "capstone" experiences encourage students to apply all they have learned in college—through general education, the major, and extracurricular work?
   - Are senior papers and projects formally presented to the college community through oral presentations?

2. **Do alumni surveys help improve the quality of the college or university?**
   - How often are alumni surveyed? How are responses used to improve the quality of the institution? Are college officials able to give specific examples?
   - Are the full results of recent alumni surveys available to prospective students?

Index

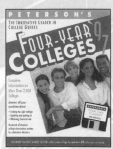